OPERATIONS MANAGEMENT

Management Executives Handbook–Series 006

OPERATIONS MANAGEMENT

U K SINGH • J M DEWAN

COMMONWEALTH PUBLISHERS
in association with
INDIAN INSTITUTE OF BUSINESS MANAGEMENT

Operations Management
Edition : 2017
ISBN 81-7169-397-0

Published by
COMMONWEALTH PUBLISHERS (P) LTD.
4831/24, Govind Lane,
Ansari Road, Darya Ganj,
New Delhi - 110002
Ph. : 23272541, 23242541
e-mail : commonwealthpublishers2016@gmail.com

Distributed by :
ARJUN PUBLISHING HOUSE
4831/24, Govind Lane,
Ansari Road, Darya Ganj,
New Delhi - 110002
Ph. : 23272541, 23242541
e-mail : arjunbooks2001@gmail.com

Laser Typesetting by :
Dimple Computers
Delhi

Printed at :
Roshan Digital Printers
Delhi

Preface

This text is designed to introduce upper-level students to the problems and techniques encountered in the operations management. Our purpose is to give future managers an understanding of the variety and importance of the management decisions faced in the operations area in different organizations, and to help them learn how to approach operations management problems. It is also our purpose to provide the foundation for further study in more specialized courses in operations management. To accomplish our objectives, the book is oriented toward problem recognition and problem solving. Several chapters use large, integrative examples to illustrate the problems that can arise in actual situations. Analytical methods are used, but their limitations and potential misuse are also stressed. The extensive examples are designed to give the student not only an understanding of the details of many operational decisions, but also a broad view of operations. We also stress the similarities and differences of operations management in different settings.

In most organizations, operations account for most of the expenditures and investments. The opportunities this creates makes operations management an interesting career, requiring an integrated view of the organization, a knowledge of marketing, finance and accounting, a knowledge of the application of mathematical and computer methods, and a high degree of interpersonal skills. We have found that an emphasis on the importance and complexity of operations management makes study in the area more enjoyable and challenging.

Editors

Contents

1 Operations Management

At the turn of the century, a number of Britons believed that every significant invention had already been recorded, and so they instituted a drive to close the Royal Patent Office. Their failure to envisage the countless new inventions developed since that time vividly demonstrates man's inability to foresee the future.

Perhaps this inability to look ahead results from the desire to keep things as they are—to maintain the status quo. The majority has never accepted change as an essential of life. When Richard Arkwright invented the spinning frame in 1769, hostile workmen attempted to destroy any replicas that appeared. Similarly, upon the introduction of steam power, many newspaper publishers urged mothers to cease bearing children because steam power would rob them of job possibilities. Nevertheless, advances in technology were adopted in the face of widespread resistance, with scores of new economic opportunities opening for the people.

In the United States, acceptance of new ideas

and adjustment to the changes wrought by innovation have occurred more readily than in most other countries around the world. But this ability to accept and adjust will be tested more rigorously in the future than ever before. The transition which overcame American society in the 1960s was merely a foretaste of tomorrow.

The change is evident everywhere. Since the end of World War II, for example, the population has increased dramatically; in November, 1967, the number of people inhabiting the United States passed the 200 million mark. Whereas it took 35 years for the population to grow from 100 to 150 million, the next 50 million was tacked on in less than half that time, namely, 17 years.

We also experienced tremendous economic growth during the 1960s. The Gross National Product increased from approximately $300 billion in 1950 to nearly $488 billion in 1960 and up to almost $750 billion in 1970. This new wealth generated dramatic increases in personal income, in consumer spending, and in the value of resources allocated for education and public welfare.

The increase in the size of institutions in this country during the same period is of great significance to the function of management. The 20 largest corporations in the United States had combined sales of over $139 billion in 1970—a volume larger than the entire Gross National Product in 1940. Similarly, public organisations greatly expanded their operations. By 1967, one out of every six nonagricultural employees had a job at some level of the government. In 1967, federal, state, and local governments were by far the largest customers in the United States, buying $176.3 billion worth of goods and services, or twenty-two per cent of every dollar spent. The size of giant private and public organizations often defies comprehension, and the growth continues.

Although we are living in an age of intense social change and unrest, many of the problems in our society are not unique to this age. In the mid-nineteenth century, every major city of the United States had slums so horrible that, in comparison, our contemporary slum areas appear benign. By 1900, New York's traffic problems with the brewery drays, horse trolleys, hackney coaches, and steam locomotives had reached a crisis. Many large cities had areas where anarchy or gange rule went unchallenged. And the history of American cities is replete with accounts of epidemics caused by polluted drinking water, streets made impassable by snow or mud, strikes and riots, and operating inefficiencies and corruption in city government.

In the eighteenth century, when the plight of the poor in Ireland became intolerable, jonathan Swift suggested, in "A Modest Proposal", that if the rich would fatten and eat the children of the poor both food and population problems would be solved. With the resources and know-how available today, Jonathan Swift would be able to suggest more reasonable solutions. For the first time, we are acknowledging the existence of such problems, and we are aware of the urgent need to solve them. The situation presents us with a tremendous challenge and opportunity. Imagine the excitement in redesigning urban centers to rid them of pollution and slums, in creating new economic opportunities to reduce poverty and increase the standard of living, in designing new transportation systems to accommodate the increasing number of travelers, and in developing the knowledge and the means to explore unknown areas of the universe.

The immediate task of our society is to marshall resources to solve these problems—to create public and private institutions which can achieve social and economic goals in the most effective and efficient manner possible. We must structure organizations of the future to accommodate and adjust to change, to work as a unit toward common goals, and to evaluate the performance of each of the various segments towards accomplishing the master plan.

Unfortunately, the typical functional organisation cannot meet current or future requirements efficiently. If traditional organizations had possessed sufficient flexibility, the buggymarkers of the past would have become today's automobile manufacturers, and the railroads would have used the airplane in their transportation system.

Management by system is more adaptable to change than the typical functional organisation. For this reason, we have chosen management by system as a framework for the study of Operations management. We define Operations Management as the design and operation of systems, including the application of those tools and techniques which are useful in achieving efficient and effective systems performance. Operations Management, as described in this text, has application to all forms of public and private organizations, those engaged in manufacturing, distribution, and service. A more detailed discussion of this field of study, and its relation to other subject areas, is included later in this chapter.

General systems theory

What is systems theory? What is a system? We might modify the phrase "happiness is different things to different people" and say "systems mean different things to different people". For example, some relate systems to science which they describe as a systematic body of knowledge; an array of essential principles or facts arranged in a rational dependence or connection; a complex of ideas, principles, laws, forming a coherent whole. Scientists endeavor to develop, organise, and classify material into interconnected disciplines. Two well-known works, Darwin's The Origin of Species and Keynes' General Theory of Employment, Interest and Money, represent attempts to integrate a large amount of related material. Darwin, in his theory of evolution, integrated all life into a "system of nature" and indicated how the myriad of subsystems were interrelated. Keynes, in his work, connected the many complicated natural and man-made forces that influence an economy. Both men had a major impact on man's thinking because they were able to conceptualize interrelationships among complex phenomena and integrate them into a systematic whole. The term systems, when used in this context, connotes plan, method, order and arrangement.

Similarly, general systems theory has been described as the development of a systematic, theoretical framework for describing general relationships of the empirical world. Existing similarities in the theoretical construction of various disciplines become apparent upon examination. Models can be developed that are applicable to many systems, whether physical, biological, behavioral, or social. An ultimate but distant goal of general systems theory is to develop a framework that will tie all disciplines together in a meaningful relationship.

The need for a general systems theory

One of the most important indications of the need for a general systems theory pertains to the problem of communication among the various disciplines. Although there is similarity in the general approach, the results are not often communicated across discipline boundaries. Hence, the conceptualizing and hypothesizing done in one area seldom are used in other areas even though such work might contribute to a significant breakthrough. Specialists seldom communicate with one another between disciplines. Of course, the conflict of ideas and difficulties of communication are even greater between the various fields of study—the scientific, the social sciences, and the humanistic.

On the positive side, there has been some tendency toward interdisciplinary study in recent years. Areas such as social psychology, biochemistry, astro-physics, social anthropology, economic psychology and economic sociology have been developed in order to emphasize the interrelationships of previously isolated disciplines. More recently, areas of study and research that call on numerous subfields have been advanced. For example, cybernetics, the science of communication and control, draws on electrical engineering, neurophysiology, physics, biology and several other fields. Operations research is often pointed to as a multidisciplinary approach to problem solving. Organisation theory embraces economics, sociology, engineering, psychology, physiology and anthropology. Problem solving and decision making are also becoming focal points for analysis and research, drawing on numerous fields. Unfortunately, the "new" cross-disciplines sometimes create a jargon that tends to compound the communication problem.

With such examples of interdisciplinary approaches, it is easy to understand the surge of interest in large-scale, systematic bodies of knowledge. However, this trend calls for the development of an overall framework within which the various subparts or disciplines can be integrated but in which they still retain the type of discipline that distinguishes them. The approach of providing an overall framework extracts phenomena common to many different disciplines and develops general models which include such phenomena.

Systems defined

Within the context of general system theory, we stated that a system is an assemblage or combination of things or parts forming a complex or unitary whole. In this usage it covers an extremely broad spectrum of concepts—for example, in the world around us, there are mountain systems, river systems, and the solar system. The human body is a complex organism made up of a skeletal system, a circulatory system, and a nervous system. We come into daily contract with transportation systems, communication systems, and economic systems.

An obvious hierarchy of systems can be created; systems, systems of systems, and systems of systems of systems. For example, the universe is a system of heavenly bodies, which includes many subsystems of stars called galaxies. Within one such galaxy is the solar system, one of many planetary systems. Similarly, an organism is a system of mutually dependent parts, each of which might include many subsystems. The human body is, for example, comprised of organs which are themselves subsystems of the organism as a whole.

Now we can use this same framework or philosophy in the task of managing resources. If organizational units are designed and operated as a system, each segment or subsystem can be viewed as a self-contained unit and its relationship or contribution to the next level in the hierarchical structure can be programmed and measured. This means that precise identification of units and of their input and output is an essential part of management by system. Before elaborating in greater detail, however, we should offer a working definition of systems, a definition which can be used as a basis for the study, design, and operation of man-made systems.

We will define a system *as an array of components designed to accomplish a particular objective according to plan.* This definition contains three significant parts. First, the system must have a purpose or objective to perform. Secondly, components are designed in a meaningful arrangement. Finally, inputs of information, energy, and materials are allocated according to an operating plan. This definition may be clearer when it is considered in conjunction with Figure, a model of a basic system. Planned resource inputs of information, energy and materials are transformed by men and/or machines to produce output of products, ideas, or service. This output, if the system is effective, achieves the purpose or goal of the system.

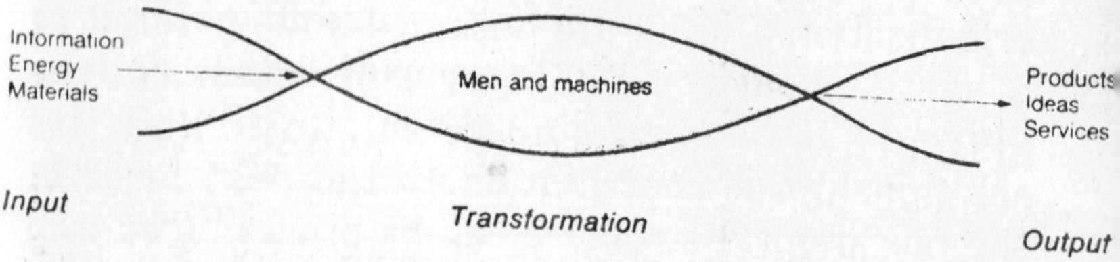

Model of a basic system

Types of systems

Systems may be classified in various ways—for example, natural systems, such as the solar system, as compared to man-made systems, such as a transportation system. Those relationships between objects and sequences of events observed in their natural setting which have meaning for us constitute natural systems. Such systems behave according to the laws of nature and their input-output relationships are predictable in a scientific sense. In contrast, man-made systems are those designed and operated by man. They utilize inputs from natural systems, but retain little of the scientific predictability found in nature, largely because man is somewhat unpredictable. *Our discussion will be limited to man-made systems.*

We may also distinguish between flexible and rigid systems. In a flexible system, the structure or design of the system is adjusting continually to maintain a balance or equilibrium between the system and its changing environment. In contrast, a rigid system is not a self-maintaining unit and its structure does not adjust, at least not in the short run. Most life forms, as well as economic, political and social systems are examples of flexible systems. A highway is an example of a rigid system—once constructed, little could be done in the short run to adjust to a change in traffic.

Man tries to build some flexibility into every system he constructs. For example, a building might be designed so that it could be converted to some other use if the primary need for the structure changed. The reader should not confuse flexible and rigid systems with open and closed systems.

Another classification of systems pertains to the degree of human involvement in relation to the machine. At one end of the spectrum we can visaulize a system utilizing few, if any, machines or tools. A group of natives weaving straw hats illustrates manual system of production. At the other extreme, an automated refinery programmed to produce petroleum products without human involvement during the transformation process is an example of an automatic-machine system. The man-machine relationship in most systems falls somewhere between the two extremes. Some industries have a high capital investment in machines, whereas in others the human factor is more significant.

The classifications natural versus man-made, flexible versus rigid, and man versus machine have all pertained to the design or structure of systems. The nature of a system's output forms another grouping: (1) systems that produce things, and (2) systems that serve clients. The manufacturing department of the Chevrolet Division of the General Motors Corporation is a subsystem of that corporation which is designed to produce automobiles. Man and machines follow predetermined instructions to achieve the operating goals outlined by the company. The essence of a producing organisation or system rests in the processes by which resources are converted or transformed into output.

The fundamental purpose of other systems is to serve clients. Service may be performed by distributing products, ideas or providing utility for people in general. For example, a retail store does not produce a product per se, but makes goods available to customers and therefore produces a service. Similarily, a doctor or lawyer produces a service by providing medical or legal assistance for the client.

The classifications which have been presented illustrate the various hierarchies or levels of systems, and also reveal the difficulty of distinct and meaningful groupings. The classifications are presented chiefly to help the reader gain some "feel" for systems and to see the relationship between this theory and the world in which we live.

Components of systems

In many kinds of analysis the inputs and outputs of a system are more significant than the actual transformation process. We can use this "black box" approach to demonstrate the relationship between components and systems. A component is a basic unit or "black box" which performs, or provides the facility for performing, some part of the defined transformation process. There is little or no value in subdividing or describing the component in further detail, at least not in that instance. For example, a classroom building may be considered a component in an education system when there is limited value to detail the analysis of the building according to its heating system, lighting system, and so forth. A teacher may be classified as a component in a university system, even though the same individual may be described for a medical illustration as a system with several subsystems. A component cannot satisfy the total specifications of a given system, even though the component may qualify as a system in another situation or context. Moreover, a component may be a part of more than one system—for example, we are components in our economic system, and also in parallel social and political systems. The determination of what is a system, subsystem, or component occurs when the objectives of that system are determined. The need to define the system and outline the exact boundaries, turns out to be a significant advantage of the systems approach. It also should be noted that the definition of the system determines the "total system" for the purpose of operation and analysis.

Every system includes components, some of which may qualify as systems under different circumstances, and each system in turn is a subsystem of the next higher level of abstraction. The boundaries of a system will be a function of the scope of the organization or system, the extent to which control can be exercised, and/or the nature of the problem requiring analysis.

Systems and organisations

In arranging and managing the resources of an organization as a system, the achievement of goals and optimization of the input-output relationship of the total system receive primary attention. The preparation and management of a system require a sequence of decisions, each distinct but closely related to the others:

1. systems determination,
2. design and creation,
3. operation and control,
4. review and evaluation.

First, a decision is made to create a system. An entrepreneur decides to open a corner grocery store, a large aerospace organization decides to establish a missile division, or the government decides to create an agency to help solve the problems of the cities.

After the decision is made to have a system, it

must be planned—facilities are provided as required, components arranged, and people hired. This is the design stage. The grocer must find a location, build or rent a building, and facilities in some logical layout to expedite customer service, and hire and train clerical help.

After a system has been designed and created, it is ready to function. The grocery store manager, for example, will buy and sell foods and notions of various kinds to provide a service to the customer and, hopefully, make a profit.

Basic to operation by system is the premise that given certain inputs, the system will produce certain outputs, or operate within established limits. However, the relationship between structure and operation may not be predictable. A predetermined equilibrium, particularly in flexible systems, can seldom be forecast by equation, and will change, within limits, as the components of the system are rearranged, or as the inputs are allocated. In most instances, therefore, there must be control of operations, or a means of keeping the system on course in spite of unpredictable variables. Control includes a sensor for measuring output or related characteristies, a means of comparing the measurement—with a standard, and an activating unit to adjust inputs to correct any indicated deficiencies. The control should regulate the variables so that the system will tend to stabilize near an established equilibrium. This objective is possible only if a meaningful standard can be determined and if such operating values can be measured. Note the significance of feedback. First, control measures operating information and feeds it back to be compared with an established standard. When corrective action is indicated, control releases instructional information to activate a change in input.

The fourth decision level pertains to how well the system has operated. Has it been effective and/or efficient? A system is *effective* if it accomplishes its objectives, while *efficiency* is the relationship of resource input to output. A system can be effective while wasting resources, and conversely, may transform inputs efficiently without achieving the objectives as outlined. The answer is to determine a balance between effectiveness and efficiency whenever the two are in opposition. Obtaining such a balance becomes the optimal course of action and we say the system is optimized. A nonoptimal condition exists to the extent that this balance does not occur. For example, there is always a conflict between the quality of the product and the cost of production. We would try to achieve the greatest quality and still keep costs acceptable to the competitive environment.

Periodically, review and evaluation occur during the life cycle of a system, and they may lead to design changes in the present system, or recommendations for change which may be incorporated into future systems. Review and evaluation are often conducted in conjunction with the operations of a system. The feedback of operating information furnishes evidence of how the system is doing, that is, whether or not design changes are required. Such analysis may bring changes in design, whereas control action causes changes in operating input.

Inputs of information, energy, and materials are basic to all systems. *Information* is needed during the design and creation stage to determine how the stated objectives can be accomplished; *energy* exerted by people or the power to operate machines; and *materials* are transformed into the equipment and machines that will be part of the system. In operation and control, all inputs are either inputs of *information,* inputs of *energy,* or inputs of *materials.*

Planning or decision making takes place at all four stages. The kind and extent at each stage, however, will vary with the nature or kind of system. For example, an automated oil refinery must be carefully preplanned. Most operating decisions are programmed into the system. A department store establishes more general objectives and plans, and uses decision making at the operating level to adjust the system to various environmental influences which are bound to occur.

The case for a systems approach

During the past two or three decades, several concepts and theories have been proposed as a framework for the management of organizations. A brief review of some of these approaches will illustrate why we have chosen a systems approach as the general model in this book.

Information theory

Information theory, or the mathematical theory of communications, can be used to study various management situations. By making certain basic assumptions, a simplified set of mathematical relationships has been developed which is used primarily in the technical aspect of information transmission. Information theory has been applied as a methodology for determining the rate at which information can be transmitted under certain specified circumstances. Some of the factors affecting transmission include the nature of the signal source, whether the signal is discrete or continuous; the nature of the channel and, in particular, its capacity for transmitting information; the nature of the noise, if any, which disturbs the transmission; and the fidelity criterion by which the adequacy of the transmission is judged.

Although a wide range of applications is claimed for information theory, most are in the technical aspects of transmission. Some of the subdisciplines are filtering theory, detection theory, and the analysis of signals statistics. Information theory is cited as an integral part of such areas as the theory of communications, the theory of automata, the theory of automatic control systems, the analysis of language, and informational aspects of physics. Fields where information theory is cited as operative an unified are thermodynamics, statistical mechanics, photography, language, models, gambling, cryptology, pattern recognition, and computer technology.

Information flow is one of several integral systems in a business or public organization, while systems management is the overall framework within which communication or information flow fits. Communication systems, or systems of information flow, are the vehicle through which the key management functions can be integrated an administered.

Decision making theory

Many theorists have focused their attention on the *decision-making processes* within an organization. One group concentrates on the human problem-solving processes and decisions mechanisms as the primary forces in organizational behavior. According to this thesis, organizational participants should not be *viewed as mere mechanical instrumentalities, but should be perceived as individuals with wants, motives, aspiration levels, and drives*, and with limited rationality and capacity for problems solving. In other words, this theory regards people not as components but as very complex subsystems contributing to the system. The question is often raised whether the objectives of the system or those of the people participating in the system should be optimized.

Others view the field of decision making as synonymous with "managing". In this sense, decision making has three principal stages: *intelligence*-searching the environment for conditions calling for decisions; *design*-inventing, developing, and analyzing possible courses of action; and *choice*-selecting a particular course of action from the available alternatives.

Another group of theorists regard the quantitative aspects of decision making as the key to the selection, design, and operation of systems. These theorists have concentrated on developing and refining mathematical models and techniques.

Systems analysis

The systems approach may be used as the general model for designing and operating organizations, but *Systems Analysis* is a technique for planning and solving problems. As such, it becomes an orderly method used to review and appraise alternative ways of using scarce resources to accomplish a particular objective. Considering the integrative nature of a problem, the constantly changing environment in which planning must be formulated, and the limited resources and time available to complete a study, the logic of this approach can assist and refine the decision-making process.

In many ways systems analysis is very similar to the scientific method. It includes a phase in which requirements and constraints are carefully outlined, alternative methods of achieving the objectives are carefully outlined in detail, trade-off studies are made within the selection criteria for determining the best alternative, and a decision plan developed which satisfies specified objectives.

Systems analysis is problem-oriented and follows a logical process of deductive-inductive reasoning. Questions considered include:

1. How many distinguishable elements are there to this seeming problem?
2. What cause-and-effect relationships exist among these elements?
3. What function needs to be performed in each case?
4. What trade-offs may be required among resources, once they are defined?

The reasoning process always goes fom deductive to inductive as it progresses from general objectives to plans and then back in a cyclical, closed-loop fashion to redefining objectives and making more detailed plans. The process, illustrated, through several stages of development starting with general objectives and proceeding to plans, then back to refining objectives and detailing plans further, then back again, and so forth.

The four main stages-translation, analysis, trade-offs, and synthesis—are also illustrated. Translation represents the statement of the problem, including all of the constraints placed on the solution. Organizational policies prescribing general patterns of action, and time or cost restrictions placed on the design and/or operation of the system are examples of constraints. At this stage, selection criteria, such as cost/effectiveness, timing and risk, are outlined and used to evaluate the appropriateness of various trade-offs. The practical reiteration of the cycle until refinements have sharpened the final plan or solution illustrates the feedback features of the model.

At some point, a practical solution or plan may not be feasible. If this occurs, the decision makers review the objectives, along with constraints and selection criteria. A slight modification or adjustment may be the decision makers to increase the alternative solutions, or to develop feasible solutions from among the current alternatives.

Material, energy, and information flow are essential elements of any given system or subsystem, although each may be developed as a flow process itself. The design of a system may highlight any one of these elements, but it must consider all three. For example, material flow could be traced through a process flow chart. A space and layout study could determine optimal arrangements of facilities and equipment in consideration of the flow of raw materials through the system. In layout analysis the human element in the man-machine system is an extremely significant factor. Decision makers can develop organizational charts as a matrix to apply to specific systems, rather than arranging them in the traditional, functional hierarchical manner. The organization, structured around the flow of material and information between decision points, would cut across traditional, functionally specialized department boundaries. This structure focuses attention on subsystem and total-system objectives and goals.

Systems analysis has been used effectively for planning advanced systems and technologies. When used with skill and common sense, it has been a valuable technique for identifying advanced requirements of complex systems, assessing the impact of environmental changes on developmental plans, identifying potential problems in the conceptual stage of a program, and providing accurate documentation of the decisions made and the supporting reasons for recommended courses of action.

The systems approach

The systems approach is the broad framework to which such concepts as information flow and decision theory, and techniques like systems analysis relate. These various forms of analysis should not be considered separately, but as segments of something larger where each can contribute enormously to the others for "—the integrated whole is much greater than the sum of the parts. Each produces an analog of an enterprise system or subsystem, and these analogs stimulate the behavior of the system caricatured."

The systems approach is not new; it is a concept borrowed from the natural sciences. Now it is being used as a philosophy for operating organizations-inputs and outputs are identified relative to stated objectives. For students of management, this philosophy is equally valuable for organizing, classifying, and simplifying knowledge which can be applied to organizations of one kind.

To summarize, and also to establish a more formal relationship among the various usages of the term systems in this chapter, we would like to suggest that there are three different ways to consider systems: (1) systems concepts or philosophy, (2) systems management, and (3) systems analysis. All three are included under that most general classification, the Systems Approach. These relationships are illustrated in showing that systems can be used as a concept of philosophy, as a means of organizing and managing resources, and/or as a planning or problem solving technique. In every instance it is the systems approach.

Operations management and systems

At the turn of the century, Frederick Taylor published his concept of Scientific Management, emphasizing the need to organize industrial production more effectively. Several techniques such as methods study, time and motion study, planning and progress charting, and pay incentives were developed in conjunction with scientific management.

Taylor's work had a great influence on production management and on the way it was taught in colleges. For many years, the typical book in this field was organized around his philosophy and also included something about every function needed to operate an industrial concern, for example, finance, forecasting, engineering design, and personnel management. Since that time, a gradual change has taken place to exclude those general management concepts which warranted a more specialized and comprehensive coverage, and to include the more sophisticated techniques which have been developed, and to concentrate on certain basic ideas and techniques that apply to all organizations.

This broader application meant that the name, production, was somewhat inappropriate because production means manufacturing to most people. Therefore, a change in name is taking place—from production to operations management. Another problem relates to the difficulty of presenting a group of techniques without an adequate relationship to some general model. Under industrial management, the manufacturing firm was this model, but with the broader application, there was a need to change the name in order to counter the arguments that manufacturing continued to be the central core of this field of study. The systems approach solves this dilemma, because it is a general model to which the operations of any organization can be related.

We defined Operations Management as the design and operation of systems, but this definition is too broad. We shall confine our discussion to those principles which relate to the analytical consideration of resources.

The choice of subject matter for a text is

always a difficult decision. We have included those areas which apply to all systems, such as design, the scheduling of resource inputs and transformation activities, management of various types of inventory and more generally, control of operations. A question may arise, however, about such an activity as purchasing—isn't it common to all organizations? Although this may be true, much of the significant information about purchasing is institutional, and it becomes difficult to make an effective presentation of the subject matter without lengthy review of the nature and character of the items or services to be purchased and of the environment of the organization.

Throughout the book, we present models, techniques, and tools as they apply of specific applications of management. Understanding this technical part of systems analysis is important and extremely useful when the application occurs within the philosophy of the systems approach. Decisions on what systems to design, and how to design and operate them, must be made. Large systems are a composite of individual systems or nodes, linked together by various forms of communication and transportation. This total system approach involves many interesting analytical and philosophical questions of strategy and trade-offs.

The study of design and its relation to control and evaluation starts in Chapter 6. Closely related to the design function is the study of information flow, and the selection and replacement of equipment.

Simulation and industrial dynamics are demonstrated as meaningful approaches for analyzing the impact on the operation of the system caused by a variation of input combinations. Obviously, one of the most important facets of operations relates to the management of human resources. Although this input is included in the operation model, its development is left to authors specializing in that field of study.

2 Implementing Operations Research

Opening a study on the implementation of operations research (OR) with this question may seem somewhat academic; however, if the paucity of literature on the subject is any indication, it is by no means clear that its answer is affirmative to everyone. Moreover, a clear statement of the problem area of this study is certainly desirable, given the confusion that exists about the meaning of the term "implementation"—a confusion that is understandable, since even those who explicitly profess concern about OR implementation disagree about the meaning of this term.

If therefore seems prudent to start out with a provisional working definition of OR implementation. We will say that an operations research recommendation is implemented if the manager or managers affected by the recommendation adopt the research results in essence and continue to use them as long as the conditions underlying the research apply.

Implementation is obviously a matter of degree. Some modifications of an OR proposal should not be construed as its rejection; they are usually necessary. On the other hand, it should not be a foregone conclusion that implementation has been achieved if the manager's decisions turn out to be the same or very close to the ones proposed by the operations researcher. This is why the last part of our definition emphasizes adoption "as long as the conditions underlying the research apply." In other words, our definition requires at lest some managerial understanding of the research underlying the OR recommendations. Assuming rational management, our definition thus reserves the term implementation for "good" operations research, introduction of which will further management's objectives and lead to a net improvement in the organisation's operations. Poor research recommendations can be used, but cannot be implemented.

We can best clarify the objectives and the scope of the present study by delineating its boundaries:

1. Our interest does not focus on the introduction of the OR function as such by a client system. Awareness of OR's existence—although not always known by this name—is fairly widespread. Industrial surveys seem to indicate that the actual introduction of OR activity has been lagging, but these results should not be overemphasized. Traditionally OR has been conducted under many different organizational arrangement—ranging from a centralized staff function to a highly

decentralized line-connected function—and under many different names such as operations research, systems analysis, quantitative methods, or computer services. As a consequence OR activity is often not recognized as such.

A series of studies concentrating on the introduction and acceptance of OR in industry has been conducted by Rubisetein, et al. These studies highlight the relationship between OR effectiveness, the degree of acceptance of the OR activity, and the variables that determine this degree of acceptance.

The scope of our study is more limited. We will focus on the behavioral characteristics that determine if and how a specific OR proposal will be accepted by management. We will take it as given that the OR function as such has already established itself in the organization. Obviously, successfully introducing an OR function and successfully implementing a specific OR proposal are interdependent. The results of our study should therefore be qualified for and integrated with the findings in a larger framework such as Rubinstein's.

2. Neither are we at this point interested in the shortcomings of OR in its technical aspects. The extension of methodology and techniques that will allow the operations researcher to cope with more and more complicated problem situations is being studied extensively and forms the main content of the professional OR

journals at this time. We will restrict ourselves to the case in which the technical OR function has produced results, for it is only when the research can technically be called "successful" that implementation—as defined above—may arise as a problem.

We can finally return to the question raised at the beginning of this chapter. By now, one might think, the problem of OR implementation—if it exists at all—has been reduced to insignificance owing to the restrictions that we imposed on our subject matter. Some survey results should convert the doubting reader. Schumacher and Smith in their 1965 industrial survey selected 65 companies from *Fortune's* top 500: 49 of these companies reported having OR activities, but "only 2 companies reported no major problem in the implementation of the OR program."

The last statement gains still more in significance when one realizes that the McKinsey survey was heavily biased toward oil companies—recognized leaders in the use of OR—and toward companies "which seemed good prospects for OR success stories."

We are not yet in a position to evaluate the many proposed remedies to overcome the difficulties in implementing OR. But comments like the one quoted above should make it clear that relatively simple solutions, such as educating management in quantitative techniques in order to adapt the organization to the "new methods," will not be enough.

In the meantime, the uneasy feelling about OR implementation continues to increase as the gap widens between the development and sophistication of OR techniques on the one hand and the managerial use of them on the other. It is our aim to decrease the tension thus created by trying to gain insight into some aspects of the problem of OR implementation. In particular, we will be concerned with the researcher's side of the problem: what strategy should the operations researcher use to maximize the probability that optimal action on his research recommendations will be taken?

The attitude of the operations researcher toward the implementation of his recommendations

Many attempts, especially in the 1950's, have been made to specify the objectives, working area, and methods of operation research. Recognizing the diversity of views on this subject, we state the following broad definition of OR's main interest: OR pursues, by using the scientific process of inquiry, the improvement of the operation of organizations. An organization can be defined as a purposeful system with the following characteristics:

1. Some elements in the system are human beings.
2. The responsibility for the choice of acts is divided.
3. The elements in the system are interacting through communication or observation.

4. A control function, which compares achieved with desired outcomes, exists as part of the system.

Morse emphasizes the significance of the human element as part of the system that OR considers when he describes the evolvement of OR from the physical sciences and notes the difference:

In OR it isn't possible to shut the worker off in his laboratory and forget about him until he is done. The thing he is studying in, in part, the organisation itself and the executive, in a way, is part of the experiment.

A summary report of I.E. symposia sponsored by the American Institute of Industrial Engineers in 1961 confirms these views; the industrial engineer is distinguished from other engineers by his emphasis on the integration of the human being into the system and the greater utilization of the social sciences.

A logical extension of the above views leads to implementation as the final criterion to measure the success of an OR effort. This conclusion may seem straightforward, but it is certainly not as easily drawn by all in the OR profession. The following two statements are exemplary of the range of actual views:

It has been argued that the researcher is responsible for producing recommendations in applied research and that he must also assume responsibility for and leadership in carrying out these recommendations if they are accepted.

Professional personnel in OR strongly emphasize this distinction between the OR responsibility for analysis and the executive responsibility for decision.

There are several reasons why OR practitioners have often given no more than casual attention to the implementation of their research findings.

One can readily point out that the use of implementation as the criterion for measuring the success of an OR effort is not feasible operationally because of the problem of adequately measuring OR effectiveness. But, as these and the following pages should make clear, we simply cannot take the luxury of using this argument as an excuse to dismiss the implementation problem or even to diminish its importance. We can only call for more effort that will help to deal more effectively with the problems of measurement. Proponents of the implementation criterion have done so repeatedly, making it clear that no simple solution to this problem exists.

Equally serious problems stem from the consideration of the human element as part of the system to be improved. This is the question we have chosen to address in more detail in this study. Explicit recognition of the human element still leaves the operations researcher with the question how and when he should include this element in his approach to a problem. Conceivably, "human constraints" could be built into an OR model in much the same way that technological constraints are handled. However, human constraints elude the formal treatment given to technological constraints: the "black box," which should excuse the OR practitioner from considering the psychological or sociological mechanism by which a human being or group converts input into output, fails to deliver the required set of technological coefficient in this case.

"Look into the black box" is essentially the proposal of those who support the "clinical" approach as opposed to the "engineering" approach in OR. If the system includes the manager, the operations researcher should include the manager in his diagnosis of the problem situation. Hence, he should not accept the manager's statement of his problems without close examination. Indeed, this is the only stand one can take in view of the chosen criterion for successful OR performance. The level of inquiry—or what can and what cannot be considered a "black box"—is no longer an arbitrary choice once one has stated one's objectives!

The actual position taken by many in the OR profession has not been to look into the black box but to forget about the "human production function" altogether. As a prominent OR scientist once stated to us: "By concentrating on the advancement of technical OR knowledge, we should get the people cut of the system and thereby eliminate all problems of OR implementation". This attitude is encouraged by a parallel development: a fast-growing body of OR techniques provides an area of satisfaction in itself. The growing demand for specialized knowledge puts extra strains on the OR practitioner and drives him in the direction of the natural scientist, who is hardly concerned about the implementation of his research findings. The OR engineer thus becomes more and more and OR scientist. He should realize that this happens at the price of giving up, at least in part, his original objectives.

We doubt that the tremendous "pure" research effort in OR—whatever its contribution to science as wisdom- has paid off in terms of an "improved operation of the system". While OR was finding its place in the American University, it became totally preoccupied with the intriguing features of its mathematical models. Ultimately, this should benefit the efficient operation of systems. This development has not been accompanied, however, by an equal interest in the advancement of a theory of system design on the one hand and a theory of implementation on the other. The OR *practitioner* is not free to choose to deal with only one of these three aspects of his problems. His "product", unlike, for example, a compound newly synthesized by an industrial chemical researcher, cannot be handed over to a production or marketing organisation so that he can return to his "laboratory".

The social scientists Katz and Kahn have drawn their conclusion from the factual imbalance they observed in the development of OR. They equate OR with "satisficing", and see it as concerned solely with the improvement of technical operations. "Systemic research", in their terminology, refers to the study of the total system and the interaction of subsystems; but this is exactly what OR set out to do! To give up this goal not only understates OR's potential, but threatens its viability.

The new function of "implementation agent", who would bridge the gap between the manager and the purely technical operations researcher, has been proposed as a way out of the OR practitioner's dilemma. The implementation agent assists the managers directly responsible for a change in accomplishing their task. The agent, being separated from the direct management of the functions affected by the research recommendations, should be able to follow a project in all its aspects and their interrelationships, cutting through established barriers in the organizational structure wherever necessary. But to do this, his function must be strictly advisory, and to be effective as an advisor the need for his assistance should be discovered by the manager who carries the implementation responsibility. The implementation agent's immediate initiative is therefore restricted to signaling misinterpretations or shortcomings of the recommendations, observing developing conflicts and proposing possible remedies, and creating an awareness of his availability for advice.

Notwithstanding his possible usefulness, the

introduction of an implementation agent affects a symptom rather than its causes. The symptom in our case is the observed existence of an implementation gap. The implementation agent might be able to close the gap temporarily by seeing to it that the research recommendations are used. To reach the point of *understanding* use of the research recommendations, we may have to delve deeper, as we will see later on.

Ackoff provides us with two additional reasons why implementation should be of *direct* concern to the operations researcher. First of all, OR is never "value free". The manager may not know his values or he may hold incompatible ones, which makes a value-free science inoperational. In addition, "with the development of an adequate technology of problem solving, a solution carries with it the prestige of science and is interpreted as a recommendation whether or not the scientist wishes it to be so considered." Second, implementation is often the only real test of the validity of research conclusions and as such should be part of the research.

Hence, we decide to open the black box of the "human production function." It seems only natural to first turn to the social scientists for information about what we will find in it.

Theory, experiments, and case studies in the social science relevant to a study of or implementation

The new directions that social scientists have taken in the study of initiating, diffusing, and controlling change are most significant to our study. Earlier writings in sociology deal with change mainly as a process of restoring a somehow disturbed equilibrium or as a necessary condition for the existence of an equilibrium. More recently the processes that can decisively change the state of equilibrium itself have been included. A whole range of new questions arise when the framework of nonchange within which change is studied is abandoned.

A useful framework for further discussion is provided by Lewin. Lewin's field theory as a conceptual system allows us to relate to one another the different approaches to change and to highlight similarities and differences in their emphasis on parts of a bigger system. Lewin describes the relationship of the individual to a concrete situation as a field of psychological forces that jointly determine the individual's behavior, that is, the directional outcome of the individual's transactions with his internal and external environment. The individual is an equilibrium-maintaining system, but this notion of equilibrium is dynamic and based on the total situation rather than a fixed framework. What constitutes the field of forces or the "lifespace" for an individual at a certain moment is the totally of facts that influence his behavior. The lifespace thus forms a psychological reality of different dimensions of which nonpsychological elements can only indirectly, through the individual's perceptions, be a part. The psychological field of forces is more or less differentiated as a cognitive structure of regions, which forms a "tension system", the tensions are created by the counteracting forces and maintained by the negative or positive "valences" of the elements in the psychological field. When the resultant force in the field differs from zero, we have change or "locomotion", either the individual—pursuing equilibrium- will move into the direction of the driving force or a change in cognitive structure equivalent to this locomotion will take place.

Festinger's theory of dissonance elaborates on the notion of an individual as an equilibrium-maintaining system. He considers different sources of dissonance arousal and different means of dissonance reduction and is especially interested in predicting behavior in case the equilibrium has been disturbed. Ample evidence for the validity of his theory has been given. It is hard to see, however, how his theory can be used for the prediction of a *specific* response as a means of dissonance reduction outside controlled situations.

The condition for change is therefore the disturbance of the equilibrium in the psychological field. This is generally recognized as the existence of a "perceived need" as a condition for change. The field-theoretical formulation indicates that disturbance of the equilibrium is reached by adding or eliminating forces resulting in a system of higher, lower, or equal tension, depending on the type of response. The actual response chosen—locomotion or cognitive change—depends on the interrelation of forces; the relative strength of goals, the attractiveness of activities to reach goals, the probability of reaching goals by a given path, the presence of authoritative pressures, and other forces. The relative importance described to the different forces is mirrored in the existence of different approaches to the process of change, the most important distinction being between the individual-oriented and the group-oriented research.

The individual-oriented research in social psychology has concentrated on the individual's perceptions of stimuli—that is, disturbances of his equilibrium—and their effect on his attitude toward certain issues. The main hypothesis in the attitude studies is that equilibrium will be maintained between a subset of forces, in particular between the cognitive, affective, and behavioral components of attitude, and that therefore a maintained disturbance of one component will lead to an adjustment of other components to reduce inconsistencies. Support for this hypothesis in specific instances is presented by Hovland and Rosenberg. The order of communications and the organisation within each communication have been studied and used to predict specific responses, such as the acceptance of a certain opinion. The findings suggest that the probability that a certain response is chosen by an individual can be increased under certain circumstances by increasing the attractiveness of that response or by adding other stimuli. The findings of these studies have to be qualified by the fact that in a laboratory setting the presence of forces other than those controlled is often deliberately minimized; for example, in most communication experiments the subjects under study had no prior knowledge of the topic involved.

The increased awareness of the forces at interplay in creating behavior called for their measurement. Measurement techniques are a major contribution of the so-called "interactionist", whose basic hypothesis is that organizational systems are built on the interactional properties of individuals. This point of view and the added diagnostic skill of measurement appears useful in studying organizations. The new techniques made it possible to demonstrate that often neglected variables such as "interpersonal competence" from significant constraints on the effective operation of organisations. But oversimplifications are likely to appear if the limitations of this point of view are not realized; such is the case, in our opinion, when the implementation of change is made a mechanistic function of the existence of adequate controls, that is, of an adequate inter-actional system.

One of the most successful recent efforts to apply social sciences to the organizational situation deals with the stage of "unfreezing" necessary for bringing about change. The group, called a training group, is used as a medium to increase the awareness of one's own and others' perceptions of expressed behavior. The individual learns and tests new behaviors in off-the-job group meetings; he is stimulated to experiment, using feedback on his behavior given to him by the group trainer. The individual's tendency to rely on a familiar "safe" but not always appropriate behavior pattern is mitigated in the training situation by minimizing the forces of threat, punishment, or criticism that he would normally anticipate in case some chosen nonfamiliar behavior should fail. It is implied that the acquired skill of diagnosing one's own behavior results in greater flexibility and therefore more willingness to consider behavior activities unused till now. The approach leans on the primacy of the rational-level forces to which all other level forces, once recognized as such, can be subdued.

The group as a target of change builds on a rich tradition of experiments and field studies. Experiments have on the one hand demonstrated the dependence of group performance on such variables as communication network, group size, problem characteristics, and perceived status of the group. On the other hand the study of the processes at work during the operation of a group has unveiled many intermediate variables and processes that determine individual and group behaviour; group attractiveness cohesiveness and sense of belonging group norms and conformity, group leaders and followers. The significance of these forces as determinants of the individuals behavior, feelings, and beliefs has led to the suggestion that it might be easier, more effective, or even essential to gain control over the group forces to influence the individual's behavior than to try to influence his behavior in a more direct way. Several field studies used the group approach successfully to bring about change. The Hawthorne studies form the classical example of group processes—viz, morale, friendship—intervening in such "technical" relationships as that between wage incentives and productivity. Another well-known example, the Harwood experiments, shows that internalizing the source of change to a group, that is, by participation in decision making, may bring the group forces into support of the change; "Thus, although a process of guided experiences which are equally his own, a person may be reoriented so that he gradually takes on within himself the attitudes which he would not accept from others". Lawrence, in his comments on some of the Harwood experiments, emphasizes that it is not the technical change per se but the social change, by which it is accompanied, that is resisted. Social and human considerations became serious obstacles for the implementation of the technical change in Coch and French's "no-participation group." The participation method, in contrast, stressed the continuity of existing social and human relationships. Workers in the "participation group" did not perceive any social change, which explains, according to Lawrence, that no implementation problem developed. Lawrence's explicit recognition of the dual aspects of change, technical and social, is particularly significant in view of the more recent developments in change research that focus on organizations as integrated socio-technical systems.

The relative importance of specific factors that determine the effectiveness of group influencing was tested in Beanett's experiments; her conclusion were that the need to reach a decision and the degree of consensus in the final decision, rather than group discussion or public commitment, are important for its implementation.

Special mention should be made here of the Asch experiments, that, to our knowledge, give the best single illustration of the importance of group pressures for the explanation of individual behavior. Asch's subjects showed a remarkable tendency to conform to a strongly favored judgment in their environment, even if the judgment was obviously wrong.

The importance of the group task—of prime interest to the operations researcher—as a determinant of behavior tends to be neglected in view of the rich complex of group forces whose interactive play is only beginning to be understood. Homans brought task and interactions together in the relationship between his "external" and "internal" systems; the interactions required by the task are the source of explanation for the extended interactions and the resulting group forces. The interdependence of forces on different levels is clarified by his framework and is explained as a system of economic exchanges of cost and reward.

The external relations of groups in their organizational setting have had relatively little attention. Mann proposed to take account of the interdependencies of subgroups in a system by the formation of "organizational families." The organizational family would be ideally conditioned for change by presenting it with feedback of survey-results about its own performance and the performance of the greater unit in which it is embedded. The discussion of relevant information at the appropriate levels in terms of immediate experience may reveal possibilities to improve operations, while participation in the analysis and interpretation of the information would motivate the change.

A next step is to look at an organization as a socio-technical system, an idea developed by Trist and his associates at the Tavistock Institute. Recognizing the primarcy of technical change as a cultural constraint, they have convincingly argued that the introduction of each technical change should be paralleled by an adaptive social change such that the motivation for efficient performance will remain. In other words, technical improvement can only be implemented when some social constraints are respected. The social constraints reflect the findings of experimental and field research; the need for a task that can be meaningfully completed control over and responsibility for the activities related to the task, and satisfactory interpersonal relationships with those performing related tasks.

Finally, there exists a rich tradition of innovation studies in which the reference point is taken to be the innovation rather than the organization or individual. The usual approach in these studies is to correlate the time of introduction of an innovation with characteristics of the innovating individual and of his reference groups. The letter have been shown to change with the different stages, from awareness to final complete adoption, of the diffusion-process.

The change agent

It is clear that the change agent becomes a new set of forces in the changec's field. In what direction these forces will operate and how they will affect other forces depends on the strategy followed. The foregoing discussion can properly be adapted to include the change agent. The managerial perception of the change agent will be affected by the agent's status, reputation, past performance, and personality. The change agent may be perceived as having direct personal valence, using his expert and referent power as a basis for influencing, or he may influence more indirectly through, for example, the authoritative power of top management. His task is to reach the proper balance between attractiveness and approachability in order to make the situation maximally conducive to the proposed change.

Theory, experiments, and case studies on the implementation of operations research

Several case studies on the implementation of OR are reported in the literature. We will discuss some of the successes and failures and see what the interested practitioners themselves have to say about the causes of success or failure and what can be done about them.

1. *Successes in OR implementation:* Vazsonyi reports the successful introduction of new decision rules, derived with OR methods, that increased production control. He points out that at the time of starting the work, there was a widespread desire on the part of management for improvements in production control and the feeling that it was possible to do better. Apparently the researcher's analysis formed a readily accepted extension of management's thinking. The McKinsey report mentioned earlier comes to a similar conclusion in explaining the impressive success of OR approaches in the refining function of the oil industry: OR formed a logical extension of the analytical calculations that refinery engineers had made for many years and OR found, therefore, a sympathetic and understanding management. Ackoff reports that of 48 technically successful projects undertaken by the OR group at Case, only one remained completely unimplemented: in this case an organizational change in management took place. The importance of a stable top management that from the outset takes a serious interest in the OR effort is underscored by the reasons Ackoff mentions for partial non-implementation in 8 other cases: A reorganization of management, the lack of involvement of a high enough level of management, the use of research for the manager's personal rather then organizational objectives, and economic pressures that led to

abandonment of the study. The need to deal with the highest executive and with corresponding authority is also mentioned in a successfully implemented cargo containerization study for a shipping line. Weldon in particular emphasizes the importance of "selling" to convince management that the OR recommendations rest on an adequate consideration of all important factors that affect the decisions involved. It should be noted, however, that containerization was equally supported by the engineering department of the firm.

2. *Failures in OR implementation:* The failure to introduce sampling methods for the interaccount clearing system of railroads—which would have led to big savings—is reported by Churchman. Middle management was used to thinking in terms of percentage error and did not want to accept sampling for smaller populations for which the percentage error, but not the dollar error, increased.

A boxcar information system, designed to optimize the operation of boxcars for a railroad, showed potential savings of $5 million per year, but was abandoned two years after its introduction. The system itself was not the cause of the failure, however. Insufficient communication with middle management, which had arrived at its position through experience rather than formal training and was already suspicious of quantitative methods and research, created a climate of distrust and uncertainty. A lack of understanding of the new system also led to a continued one-sided policing of those instances in which shortages required the overworking of facilities, whereas surpluses were overlooked.

We not that in the two last examples lack of understanding was the major reason for OR failure. Turning once more to the literature, we find numerous determinants of OR implementation described and stressed to varying degrees. Miller and Starr emphasize the characteristics of the research proposal as determining the "degree of belief" on the part of management. On the one hand, there is the degree to which the strategy and tactics of a proposal have been specified, the degree of certainty of the anticipated outcome, and the corresponding degree of control over the outcome. On the other hand, there is the degree of commitment that is required for implementation, which differs for repetitive and nonrepetitive solutions, the degree of reversibility of a procedure once introduced, and the degree of permanence of the solution proposal. Ackoff emphasizes the relationship of the operations researcher to the manager. The operations researcher should communicate directly with the authority capable of controlling all functions involved in his research. The manager, on the other hand, should be committed to pay sufficient attention to the operations research proposal by making the research available only at a cost. However, the conditions under which research is performed are not always under the researcher's control to the extent required by Ackoff's proposal.

Top-management support for the researcher is often isolated as the critical factor by the OR profession, and it is often implied that implementation will follow automatically if the researcher is adequately backed by top management's authority. In view of the discussion in the foregoing section on the field of forces that determine managerial behavior, this view is at least naive. In the case studies we described above, implementation did not take place *despite* top management's support.

Being aware of the multidimensionality of the problem of implementation, we note that a recurring theme—as illustrated by the cases mentioned above—is the way of thinking and understanding on the part of management. Implementation appears to have been most successful in environments that are "in tune" with the analytical OR approach long before the operations researcher appeared on the scene. Miller and Starr seem to have this in mind when they say that the manager's "belief will further depend upon the extent to which the decision criterion expresses his intuition and attitudes". Churchman points to the aspect of understanding in order to explain why information together with analysis do not yet imply implementation. Understanding is also the basis for distinguishing four basic attitudes with respect to the manager-researcher relationship by Churchman and Schainblatt. As a conclusion to his study, Rogers attempts to give an outline of a "theory of diffusion and adoption of innovations." His "generalizations," indicate what is to be the body of his theory and leave no doubt about the central role of perception, the key dimension of understanding.

The small group experiments by Churchman and Ratoosh are explicitly designed to test implementation behavior. Since this study is a direct outgrowth of the Churchman-Ratoosh experiments, they deserve more attention. The most remarkable result of these experiments has been that implementation—defined to be understanding, not merely acceptance of the research proposal—was so seldom reached. Although afterward the subjects often blamed the poor communications system for their poor performance, performance was no better when face-to-face meetings were introduced between decision periods. The introduction of *more* restrictive communications did result in more expressions of concern about the underlying causal relationships of the firm's problem, but did not result in an earlier or more complete adoption of the optimal solution presented by a confederate. The mode of presentation of the optimal solution as well as the role and status of the confederate were varied in many ways. Experimental evidence gave clearest support to "sociometric status" as a variable that directly affects the implementation of the optimal solution. A strongly "chosen" confederate appeared to have fewer problems than a strongly "underchosen" confederate in getting the optimal solution adopted by his fellow team members.

The churchman-Ratoosh experiments explored a much wider range of variables than we have mentioned above. Although several variables could be identified as affectiong the implementation process, no manageable set of critical "control" variables could be located. The whole gamut of individual and group phenomena, discussed in the previous section, became an inextricable whole. The standard answer to such a problem has been to tighten experimental controls, which at some point *inescapably* leads to clear results in the form of causeeffect relationships. There is no doubt that these relationships are worth studying. However, to decide *in what direction* control ought to be increased is to decide the implementation problem at the outset. It would mean to equate a study of implementation with a study of leadership, of conformity, of influence, or whatever aspect one chooses to consider. Churchman and ratoosh chose not to focus on some specific aspects, but to continue their exploratory effort. Elsewhere, Churchman gives an explicit justification for this approach. Talking about solipsism, he states: "The implied strategy is one of starting with simple, well-defined problems and working up to complicated ones, but how can one know which simple problems provide the correct starting points without having some idea of the nature of complicated problems and their solutions?".

3 A Behavioural Science Perspective on Operational Research Practice

The main argument is that the relationship may be thought about at three fundamentally different levels.

At the first level behavioural science can be conceived as a 'tool' discipline to Operational Research, to be looked to for help, for example, in finding ways of persuading clients to value, accept and implement OR solutions.

At the second level behavioural science and OR can be thought of as intellectual and professional disciplines with overlapping interests, which can have a dialogue and debate about matters of mutual interest. Each discipline may, for example, offer alternative accounts of the same phenomena, particularly where they concern the behaviour of people in an organisational setting. There may be genuine intellectual frontiers between the two broadly conceived disciplines, of which artificial intelligence, managerial decision making and expert systems may be examples. Finally, to the extent to which either or both claim to be multi-disciplinary, it is possible to consider the extent to which each area already incorporates some of the insights of the other, or the extent to which both draw on common academic and professional sources.

At the third level OR, both as an academic discipline and an area of professional practice, can be considered as a phenomenon that behavioural science can look at, interpret, and raise critical questions about. Thus questions can be asked about the social significance of the instigation, evolution and growth of OR, and the eras, cultures and organisational settings where this has and has not happened. Questions can be asked about the values and ideologies that are built into and supported by OR. Questions can be asked about the implicit and explicit assumptions concerning the nature of both people and organised activity which underlie OR theory and practice. And, to the extent to which reality is, at least in part, 'socially constructed' as many behavioural scientists argue it is, then the question of the kind of personal and organisational realities created by OR practice can be asked. In addition, the behavioural scientist can pose questions about the kinds of people who become OR practitioners, the nature of their careers, how OR is organised within itself and within work organisations, and how its practitioners acquire and use power.

The stance underlying this paper is that each of these perspectives is valuable and useful. However it is the author's observation that operational researchers tend to prefer the first of these levels, and behavioural scientists the last, and that dialogue is less fruitful without agreement about the level or levels at which to conduct it. This is an extension of the phenomenon, observable amongst the protagonists of all disciplines claiming relevance to management, organisation or business, in which dialogue is based on the rival claims that 'my discipline includes/interprets/is "meta" to, your discipline'. Resisting the temptation to fall into this trap, and the very real difficulty in doing this, is a major challenge to inter-disciplinary cooperation, and suggests that the middle level may be the most fruitful starting point from which to reach out to the other two.

The main aim of this paper is therefore to map some of the issues, ideas and dilemmas at each of these three levels, as an aid to thoughtful dialogue between behavioural scientists and operational researchers.

The remainder of this paper will therefore consist of a discussion of issues at each of the three levels. To make such a discussion possible it will be necessary to make a number of assumptions about what is meant by both OR and behavioural science, both of which are likely to be contentious issues. To make the discussion possible these assumptions will be stated briefly before the discussion of the three levels.

Assumptions about the nature of operational research

The naive reader approaching the OR literature to see what it is all about gets a reasonably consistent picture of what, at its conventional core,

OR is. It is concerned with being 'scientific' about problems that exist in a 'real' operational world, usually with some notion of optimisation being applied, through various techniques, to manipulate a model, usually mathematical, of the problem situation, and decide a 'best solutions'. Such is the flavour of basic definitions offered by much quoted authors such as Churchman.

The notion of what is 'scientific' seems to be, very much as Checkland says, based on an image of empirical natural science, giving much emphasis to objectively observable, preferably quantifiable, phenomena. There is a high degree of consistency in the historical accounts of OR, which fits with this picture, of its having its origins in war time efforts to make radar work in the field by generalising the scientific method of technical research on radar to the study of systems within which radar was used.

The historical account of OR also reveals two interesting points for the purpose of this discussion. Firstly there is an early emphasis on interdisciplinarity, both among different fields of science and across to practitioners in the form of professionals and managers. Scientists were seen as providing method, with their substantive knowledge being incidental, while the professionals and managers knew and had influence over the problem. It is interesting to note, however, that the example quoted by Beer of a wartime group centred on Professor Blackett included 'another physicist, three physiologists, a surveyor, two mathematical physicists, an army officer and an astro-physicist', behavioural science being notable for its absence, although this was the era in which behavioural science, particularly in its more psychological forms, was growing rapidly in its applied usage in the military context. More recently the multi-disciplinary feature has faded out of accounts of OR, in favour of a view of OR as a discipline in its own right, with applied mathematics, modelling and optimisation as its substantive and methodological core.

The second point of historical interest is the early claim to find observable stable patterns of events even where these are 'rather unexpected in view of the large number of chance events and individual personalities and abilities that are involved in even small operations'. This statement, of observable mathematical regularities in aggregated events involving people, seems to constitute the standard OR justification for not needing to grapple with the confusing variety of behavioural science thought.

Assumptions about the nature of behavioural science

Behavioural science presents no such unified central concepts, methods or history, though many strands of all of these are inentifiable, and the history longer. The label is immediately problematical both in the terms 'behavioural' and 'science'. The safest statement to make may be the most common senesical: that behavioural science is the study of people.

The broad traditional categories of approach

are probably still the psychological and the sociological, but with other long standing disciplines like anthropology in attendance, intermediate disciplines like social psychology, new disciplines like linguistics, hybrids like 'organisational behaviour', which has tended to become the standard label in management and business school curricula, particularly American ones, and areas of professional practice like organisational development, all making up a complicated and messy picture. The term 'behavioural' may tend towards the psychological end of the spectrum, and even bridge out into physiological explanations of behaviour. The term 'social', as in 'social science' may emphasise the other end of the spectrum—concerning people in the collective sense, and that meanings the individuals attach to themselves, their actions and institutions surrounding them.

One assumption or belief shared by much of behavioural/social science is, stated simply, that there is more to people and what they do than can be explained by their material make up and organic biological processes. It is because of this, primarily negative statement, that the issue of what it means to be 'scientific', and all the methodological and philosophical issues that follow from this, is more complicated and contentious in the behavioural sciences than it appears to be in OR. As an extension of this, a mutual non-acceptance of what the other regards as scientific, and on the behavioural side, not being able to present a clear consensus on methodology anyway, may be one of the major blocks to comprehension and dialogue.

The empirical natural science model adopted by OR represents one approach used in the behavioural sciences, characterized as the logical positivist approach when viewed from a philosophical perspective, and manifesting itself in experimental design approaches copied from natural science, biology, clinical trials and agricultural research. Strong arguments have been mounted against this approach, along the general lines, greatly simplified, that this degenerates behavioural science back to the biological and material, and that an appropriate methodology must allow for the reality of the non-material or biological, such as subjective experience, social process, patterns of meaning and symbolism. However in some areas of the behavioural sciences, this argument has been won well in the past, in others it has scarcely been heard.

If a general statement about what behavioural science means by being scientific can be risked, it is perhaps that the method must be open to, and appropriate for, the kinds of phenomena that behavioural science theories can postulate, about the nature of what is human over and above the physical and physiological. This may involve a much broader conception of what is acceptable empirical evidence, and it may entail non-empirically based analysis of the nature of theories themselves and the ways in which it is possible to conceive human processes.

Behavioural science as a tool for OR

The basic hypothesis of this paper is that OR is confident enough of its own essentially non-behavioural science general aim and approach to prefer to see behavioural science as a peripheral tool rather than a core interdisciplinary contributor, or a radical critic.

There appear to be two main areas of contribution for behavioural science as a tool within the classical OR investigation: contribution of concepts, models and measures within the investigation, and dealing with the client system before, during and after the investigation.

Within an OR investigation it may seem desirable to include some behavioural variables, while staying with the basic concept of a quantifiable model of a met of causally related variables, making possible the calculation of an optimal arrangement. Within a manpower planning model, for example, it may be necessary to use such variables as 'morale' and 'job satisfaction' as determinants of labour turnover, 'skill' as a determinant of performance, 'learning curve' as a predictor of growth of performance over time. In such an investigation behavioural science might be looked to first to suggest the variables, second for hypotheses about how they might fit into the model, and thirdly for empirical methodologies for measuring them.

A survey of the use of 'behavioural' variables in OR models is well beyond the scope of this paper, but two casual hypotheses might guide such an investigation: firstly that OR will avoid behavioural variables wherever possible, and second, where they are used they will be borrowed most readily from areas of the behavioural sciences that have stayed closest to the 'natural science' model of doing research.

Shilton provides an example of the former; in a model to predict demand for train services he uses a variable Q for 'quality of service', which he defines operationally as a function of speed and frequency of service, rather than as a behavioural variable rooted in the experience of the railway passenger, and to be assessed empirically.

An example in support of the latter hypothesis is provided by Polding and Lockett in their attempt to study a phenomenon associated with the second part of this section: implementation of OR projects. This study does grasp the empirical nettle and attempts to assess the experiences of practioners and clients through questionnaire survey. However the analytical methods of principle components and regression analysis are immediately called in to give a reassuring, if possibly spurious, sense of order to this data, and present it in a form more compatible with the normal OR model. Such data-raking techniques are mainly used in those branches of the behavioural sciences that feel the need to convert their data into quantitative expression of quasi-causal relationships. It seems significant to this author that such an approach was used in preference to in depth qualitative case studies of a smaller number of OR studies from instigation to implementation.

Although, as stated above, the conventional core of OR seems clearcut, there is an apparent sense of 'crisis' in some people's minds which appears, in the first instance, to be a crisis of mismatch between theory and practice, rather than within the theory itself. To the extent to which the crisis is real, there seem to be two responses to it. The first is that the problem is, after all, a substantive and theoretical one, and that OR needs to shift its theoretical base in a systems/cybernetic direction. The second is that the OR core is basically sound, and the crisis derives from a mismatch between the rational logic of OR and the less rational psycho-logics of the processes involved in the acceptance and implementation of OR solutions. In this view it is the applied behavioural science of the consultant interaction with client systems which holds the key to overcoming the crisis, and actually describes what the day to day work of the OR practitioner is like, in contrast to that which is implied by the OR curriculum. This is therefore the area in which OR practitioners may be most ready to look for help from behavioural science tools.

Such help is on offer from some branches of the behavioural sciences, particularly those concerned in the broadest sense with organisational development, see for example Lippitt and Lippitt and Schein.

The general theme of such advice is that clients need to be regarded is people rather than rational decision making machines simply needing a correct technical solution. Some of the kinds of points that arise are:

(1) Understand the problem the client sees, and how they see it, and talk to them in their language.

(2) Recognise the nature and limits to the power and authority of the client.

(3) Be sensitive to the pressures on the client, and their needs to maintain their own sealf-esteem.

(4) Recognise that clients may be more able to take on new ideas at some times rather than others, and can sometimes do this only slowly.

(5) Recognise that clients can either be 'complacent' about a problem or in a quiet state of panic about it—the former need the reality bringing home to them, the latter need encouraging to see that there are solutions and ways out.

(6) In attempting to get a problem recognised and a solution accepted, consider the questions; *who knows* about the problem, *who cares* whether it is solved or not, and *who can* do anything about it. If an overlap between these categories exists or can be brought about, then this may define a fruitful client to work with.

(7) Try to put forward solutions and recommendations that are not only *technically sound* but also *politically acceptable* and *administratively feasible.*

(8) For a client to take action he or she needs to *recognise a problem,* have a *vision of its solution, see a path to this solution,* and know in detail the *first step* in this journey.

(9) Clients are likely to grow to trust consultants only slowly, as they prove trustworthy, reliable, helpful and sensitive—initially over small matters.

(10) A consultant can usefully give a client a balance of *support* through listening and sympathy about a problem and *confrontation* with evidence of new aspects of the problem, analyses or interpretations of it and ideas for ways to solve it.

Such 'practical guidelines', while being offered by some branches of the behavioural sciences may well be criticized by others as untested folk-lore, manipulative, or undermining the true role of behavioural science. However, since any consultant is likely to be a behavioural-scientist-in-practice, points like the ten above may at least provide a starting point for becoming more aware of some of the processes involved.

The underlying principle of most of these points is about understanding the psycho-and socio-logics of the client situation. Where this problem has been addressed from within the OR transition, it has been on the basis of the concept of 'mutual understanding'. Polding and Lockett marshall a certain amount of evidence to support the view that when 'mutual understanding' is egocentrically interpreted to mean getting clients to think and understand solutions in OR terms, then this is counterproductive in terms of implementation. They conclude that 'there is possibly a need for mutual understanding more in a sociological than an intellectual sense'.

Behavioural science and operational research as adjacent disciplines

Given the pluralistic nature of the behavioural sciences, the easiest areas for substantive dialogude appear to occur where there are similar methodological assumptions.

The 'natural science' OR model would see prediction and control as major aims of this form of science, aligning it closely with technical objectives of manipuating material entities to the aims of human kind. Much of behavioural science can be seen as concerned with explanation rather than prediction and control, and with such powers of prediction and control as do arise from explanation serving the ends of individual self-control by actors in a situation, rather than control by a centralised 'human engineering' function. Thus explanation serves illumination and emancipation rather than centralised control.

Areas of common interest between behavioural science and OR appear to be limited to:

(1) behavioural science concepts that can translate into variables of the kind acceptable to OR models.

(2) methodological issues, at the level of research design and statistical, particularly multivariate, analysis.

(3) the substantive area of decision making.

Concepts and variables like 'morale', 'job-satisfaction', 'skill' and 'learning curve' were given as examples of areas of common interest in the 'behavioural science as tools' section. Such concepts, their meaning and the interpretation of empirical observations about them can potentially also be an area of inter-disciplinary discussion, though examples are hard to find. Some branches of the behavioural sciences, like research on managerial effectiveness, and leadership style seek to develop models in the OR style which identify and measure independent variables, like 'participativeness', and relate them to, and evaluate them against, measures of 'productivity' and 'performance'. Even here, however, interdisciplinary debate seems more potential than actual.

Methodological common interests may be more obvious, but only seem to occur in the parts of the pluralistic behavioural science scene that overlap the home territory of OR theory and practice. Overlaps occur at the levels of research design, and of analytical technique. Some behavioural scientists and operational researchers see themselves as having similar problems in investigating the causal relationship between variables in many variable situation which lends itself more easily to study in the field rather in a controlled laboratory setting. Issues like those of experimental design may represent common ground. Equally, at the level of analytical technique, some behavioural scientists, particularly psychometricians, would find much common ground with some operational researchers' on issues of regression analysis, factor analysis and so on.

Given that OR is in many ways defined by its methodology rather than the substantive phenomena that it investigates, and that it is presented as a practical, problem solving activity, it is clear that decision making itself, as a phenomenon of mutual interest, is in a special category. OR interest in decision making is rooted in the normative and rational, whereas the behavioural science interest is likely to be more descriptive and psychological. However the situation may be similar to the common but different interests of the computer scientist and psychologist in artificial intelligence. Both parties are interested in an operational clarification of the concept of intelligence, and both look to the other for hypothesis about proceses and mechanisms underlying it.

Studies like those by Newell and Simon. Clarkson, approach decision making from the descriptive, behavioural side, but seek to develop models in the systematic form characteristic of the normative. With the emergence of 'expert systems' there appears to be a genuine area of common interest, and a practical incentive to explore it, between the computer scientist, operational researcher and psychologist.

It is possible that areas such as this will allow a renascence of multidisciplinary OR.

A number of strands of thinking in the behavioural sciences, at a more theoretical level, are converging on the issue of human agency—the sense in which people can create new meanings, make free choices, initiate actions, rather than act out parts in a deterministic story. This suggests that the traditional OR view, that if there are regularities in aggregate events then underlying behavioural processes can be avoided; could usefully be reconsidered.

In summary, therefore it seems that:

(1) The multidisciplinary base of OR never had a high behavioural science content.

(2) What there was has eroded away as OR has become a discipline in its own right.

(3) Areas of common interest are: (i) methodological (ii) in decision making.

(4) The emergence of 'expert systems' may provide the practical incentive and pressure to address behavioural issues directly.

(5) The evolution of thought in the behavioural sciences suggests that this could be a good time to look at the question of individual 'free' choice and regularities in aggregate behaviour.

Behavioural science views of operational research as a phenomenon

Behavioural science views of OR can be conveniently organised under two headings: views of OR as an institution and a social phenomenon, and views on operational researchers, as people, and the way they are organised as a profession.

Considering OR in a historical context, it can be asked why OR sprang up and grew when it did, and where it did, and what its significance is in social history. It seems possible to discern an era of 'scientific rationality' in the two or three decades following world war II, in the West at least, corresponding to a decline in religious and spiritual values, an increase in materialistic values, an increasing influence of formal organisation on everyday life, and a corresponding decrease in the influence of family and community, all supported by the belief that science would produce solutions to all human problems. The 'crisis' in OR can be interpreted as the beginning of the end of that particular ear, and the beginning of the current one, of which the pattern is not yet clear, but which seems to contain a recognition that matters are decided by political process, reference to ideology and dogma, and various forms of fundamentalism, either religious or secular, and politically oriented 'think tanks' displace detached scientific advisers as the shapers of policy. The interesting question is, how is OR reacting to this new era?

Looking at OR from a behavioural science perspective in less global terms traises a whole series of issues about the implicit and explicit assumptions that OR makes about the nature of organisations.

It seems clear that the OR approach fits best with functionalist/systems views about organisations, as opposed to interactionist/ humanist ones. Thus organisations are seen as 'designed mechanisms' with unitary objectives and structures independent of people, rather than evolving social structures emerging from human interaction, satisfying multiple needs and objectives for multiple stakeholders. Most OR studies involve the notion of a global, collective objective function which can be optimised for maximum payoff by the right arrangement of the sub-systems causing this payoff. Thus 'payoff' is seen as the property of the abstract global entity known as the 'organisation', rather than something that accumulates to a multiplicity of people in a multiplicity of forms.

It can be argued that functionalist/systems views of the nature of organisations are self-fulfilling, in the sense that organisations behave in this manner if enough of the people in them see them this way. OR practice can be seen to support this process, and add to the centralisation of power in as much as OR projects are sponsored by, and serve the ends of, those most powerful in defining objectives, functions and structures.

At a more micro level, OR can be seen to favour objective material criteria rather than possibly more meaningful subjective ones, and thus have an effect on organisational life. For example, OR studies of hospitals are more likely to address themselves to bed-occupaney rate, cure-rate, waiting list time, than to attempt to assess human suffering and welbeing.

From a behavioural science point of view, therefore, OR, considered across the spectrum from macro to micro issues concerning its practice, represents a value position, has its own ideology, reinforces certain material, structural and power realities in organisations, and thus has a moral and either content.

Finally, behavioural science can offer interpretations of phenomena to do with operational researchers, and the ways they are organised. The personalities, careers, professionalisation and education of operational researchers, the way in which the profession is organised, and the way in which OR consultancies and departments are organised within themselves and within work organisations are examples of some of the issues that could be addressed.

The extent to which OR as an occupation attracts and selects people with certain personalities, the extent to which OR provides lifelong careers, and the 'career anchors' of OR practioners could be investigated. The extent to which OR is a profession, and exhibits the phenomena of professionalisation; claims to protect the public, maintenance of ethical standards, regulation of entry to the profession, exploitation of monopoly power, operation of a labour market, and the fixing of fees, could also be explored.

The organisation of OR consultancies and the extent to which they are organised as commercial companies or on the model of professional partnerships, must be of interest, as is the issue of how OR departments are organised and located within work organisations.

Finally, the education and training of operational researchers suggests itself as a topic of some interest. The question of a gap between theoretical and practical OR is pertinent here, as are questions of the role of education in licensing, formally or informally, practitioners as well as developing appropriate skills. Finally, the education of operational researchers could be considered from the point of view of its role in creating and maintaining the value system and ideologies implicit and explicit in OR practice.

4 Evaluation of Operating Systems

In analyzing some operating systems the objective of achieving a specific level of performance may be stated in terms of minimizing the cost or value of inputs required to achieve desired output. Consider a military logistics system which must have a certain capability to deliver material to multiple destinations. At different times in the operation of such a system, various types of questions must be analysed. For example, at one point in time, we may wish to examine alternate transportation forms. At another time, capacities of facilities may be the principal issue. At still another time, the design or redesign of the entire system may be possible. Since no one form of analysis is suitable for all situations, constraints on possible solutions and the appropriate form of any necessary models must be determined unqiuely.

A small logistics system consisting of a single base supply point at node 1, two forward areas at nodes 3 and 4 with certain material requirements, and a proposed forward supply point at node 2.

The system requires a delivery of either 20,000 units of material to node 3 or 40,000 units to node 4 within a specified time. Delivery can be accomplished either by direct movement by air from node 1 or by ground and water transportation from stocks maintained at a forward supply point at node 2. Between nodes 1 and 3, each aircraft can deliver 500 units within the specified time between nodes 1 and 4 each aircraft can deliver 1200 units within the specified time. Fifty cargo aircraft are available which cost $1 million per year per aircraft to maintain in readiness. Yearly cost of operating the forward supply point together with maintaining adequate ground and water transportation capacity to meet delivery requiremnets to either node 3 or node 4 is $1000 per unit.

Maximization of return

Conversion operations for transforming raw materials into finished products are often most appropriately analysed using an objective of maximizing return or profit. In the short run, a firm, such as a timber company or an oil company, may find that raw material supply and conversion capacity are available within upper bounds and that the firm must decide how best to utilize these resources. Typically, the firm can manufacture a range of products and can direct the flow of materials to alternate conversion facilities so that different end products are obtained. Under these circumstances the objective is to maximize return within the constraints imposed by raw material availability, conversion capacity, and size of markets.

A hypothetical system of conversion operations. In an actual case, we might have more raw materail inputs and many more products. Raw material availability, capacity, size of marekts, and technical characteristics of the conversion process all limit the flow through the system. We assume no limits on the capabilities of transportation links in the system, although we could include limits, if desired.

System response

Not all system operations are succeptible to optimization using monetary criteria. We may also indirect analysis towards developing a model that is useful in understanding the behaviour or operating characteristics of a system.

The diagram shows the general flow of criminals through the system with some individuals feeding back through the system. We may question the relevance of optimization to the analysis of this system. However, we can construct a simulation model of the system which will enhance our understanding of the behavior of the system and estimate probable effects of any changes made in it.

Simulation models may take either of two forms. They may be micro simulations which simulate on an individual basis or macro simulations which deal with the total numbers passing throught the system. We prefer the macro version since the observation of hundreds of thousands of individuals would consume too much computer time.

A simulation of the criminal justic system written in DYNAMO, one of the special computer languages conceived for such purposes. DYNAMO takes a model written in equation form and moves it ahead in a simulated period of time. The elements of the model are recomputed for each length of simulation desired, DT, and the results are printed and plotted to show the values of the items of interest throughout the entire run of the simulation.

System cost effectiveness

Operations which cannot be evaluated in terms of clear-cut monetary objectives may often be approached through cost-effectiveness calculations. Although cost-effectiveness analyses do not lead to optimizing solutions, they may provide an understanding of the operating characteristics of a system, which may be helpful in assessing alternative methods of operation. We will illustrate one type of cost-effectiveness study with an analysis of a statewide liberary system.

Public libraries typically are operated as local system supported and controlled by city and country governments. Since libraries vary widely in size, local library resources are distributed unevenly when we consider the number of volumes immediately available to the user. To make additional resources available, inter-library loan arrangements have developed which permit some sharing of resources among libraries. Usually, however, inter-library loans are slow; they function through very loose organizational arrangements, and lack comprehensive catalogs of materials in all libraries.

One suggestion for improving the present situation is to develop formal library networks across wider geographic areas to provide rapid inter-library loans and more extensive sharing of materials. As an illustration of how we may evaluate such proposals at least in an overall fashion, let us examine two alternate systems proposed for a state. In one of these systems, local libraries would be organized into regional groupings to facilitate sharing of resources within the region. The largest library in the region would be the central point in the regional network. The other proposed system is a state-wide network with all libraries linked to the largest library in the state.

The data has been tabulated by region and for the state as a whole. We assume that the regional groupings of libraries are not at issue in the analysis, being largely predetermined by natural geographic, economic, and political factors. Since there is no natural measure of effectiveness for the system, one must be constructed which is both credible and calculable from available data. We define the measure of system effectiveness as the number of persons served multiplied by the number of volumes immediately available to each person. For the present system of individual libraries, volumes immediately available are those in the local library: for the regional system volumes immediately available are those in the region; and for the statewide system, volumes immediately available are all volumes in the state. Admittedly the measure is crude and very broad, but it does provide a starting point for evaluating the alternate systems and can be refined later in the analysis.

For the present system the measure of effectiveness $\mathbf{E}_p$ is defined as:

$$E_p = \sum_j \sum_i p_{i,j} v_{i,j}$$

where i refers to the library, j refers to the region, $p_{i,j}$ is the population served by the ith library and the jth region, and $v_{i,j}$ is the number of volumes in the ith library in the jth region. For the network with regional grouping of libraries, system effectiveness E_r is

$$E_r = \sum_j (\sum_i p_{i,j} \sum_i v_{i,j})$$

And, for a network with all libraries linked to the largest library, system effectiveness E_s is

$$E_s = \sum_j \sum_i p_{i,j} \sum_j \sum_i v_{i,j})$$

The measures of effectiveness found may be criticized on several counts. The calculations assume that any book in a regional or statewide network is immediately available to any patron in that region or state. This, of course, is not the case since even a very efficient network operation using rapid communication and data processing equipment would still result in some delay, although not as substantial as with the present inter-library loan procedures. Another major criticism is that the calculated measures of effectiveness are based on the implicit assumption that all books in the system are different, whereas a great deal of duplication both within and between libraries exists in the system. Finally, the measures do not take into account the quality of the books available; a factor of great significance in a library system.

These criticisms argue that the proposed systems are not as effective as the calculations would indicate; therefore, the calculated measures of effectiveness should be viewed as upper bounds on potential system effectiveness. Although accurate measures are desirable, even an upper bound may be helpful since alternatives which appear ineffective in this most favorable context will certainly not be viable when the measure is refined.

Let us now compare effectiveness with the costs of the alternative systems. Suppose that operation system will cost $50,000 per year, whereas the statewide system will cost $800,000 per year because of greater communications costs and the need for more sophisticated data processing procedures. We may calculate benefit-cost ratios as follows:

	Additional benefits	Additional costs	Benefit/Cost
Present vs. regional system	1,280,851	$ 50,000	8.5
Present vs. statewide system	8,807,958	800,000	11.0

The statewide system, although more expensive, has the higher benefit to cost ratio and appears to be the preferred alternative at this point in the analysis. Note, that further refinements of the measures of effectiveness would be required before making a final decision.

In contrast to the other approaches we have discussed, the analysis of library operations relies much less heavily on formal model building. Rather, data which are available are used to gain a better understanding of the effectiveness of proposed alternatives. The emphasis is less on formal mathematical structure and more on devising measures of effectiveness and ways of approaching a problem which lacks data and has an inadequate structure.

5 Role of Operational Research in Corporate Planning

Introduction

It is a traditional feature of papers in this field to begin with a discussion on the definition of corporate planning. However there are as many definitions of corporate planning as there are of other management sciences such as marketing and even operational research. It would be quite easy to fill thirty pages discussing these definition alone. Drucker's contribution.

> "A continuous process of making enterpreneurial decisions systematically, and with the best possible knowledge of their futurity; organising systematically the effort needed to carryout these decisions; and measuring the results against expectations.

Provides a typical practical example. For reference, other notable and varied contributions include Taylor, Denning, Cantley, P.A. Management consultants and Howitz provides a useful conceptual critique of corporate planning with reference to some of these common definitions. At this stage it is important to recognise two different activities emerging from these definitions:

1. strategic decision making
2. tactical analysis

These two activities are not distinct—in making the decision about "what the organization does", it is necessary to have an awareness of "what resources are available and how they might be applied". If the strategy is designed to achieve the objective then the tactics are designed to achieve the strategy.

From the varied definitions there has been considerable debate as to whether corporate planning is activity, (1) activity (2) or both. Those pioneering to establish corporate planing as a new and pure individual subject tend to activity (1)- strategic decision making - on the grounds that the issues within activity (2) are not peculiar to corporate planning and have established descriptions else where-forecasting, capital budgeting, project evaluation, etc. On the other hand, if an organisation has a "corporate planning department then the people employed are most likely occupied in activity (2)- economic, business analysts, marketing specialists, accountants, operational research—number gathering "crunching". It is difficult to argue that those people are not "corporate planning". In most organisations, it is the policy making board of directors that undertakes the strategic decision making—not the corporate planning department. An appreciation of these ideas is important in examining and projecting the role of operational research incorporate planning.

Corporate planning and operational research-The past

In the sixties and early seventies, operational research become involved in tactical analysis, building financial models "with barehands" using primitive tools and dabbling with new packages. As the significance of financial modelling emerged, the popularity of the systems grew, operational research lost its dominances the main modelling contributor. The bridgehead for the continuing contribution of operational research to corporate planning was weakened for the three reasons summarised below.

1. O.R. suffered from the debate and uncertainty as to whether financial modelling etc. was really corporate planning.
2. the body of pure O.R. practitioners, worshipping the god of optimisation, frowned upon the mathematical trivialities of such activities as financial modelling
3. there was a tremendous surge of development in both modelling tools and education for other management disciplines this removed a large part of the O.R. skill in model building.

In 1973, from a survey of practitioners in model building for corporate planning, and Wooler report that 30% were operational research. From 1973 to 1982 their activity incorporate modelling increased by 6% whilst accountants have increased their activity in corporate modelling by

50% and it is apparent today that operational researchers now have limited unique tools to general corporate planning problem and that they have not maintained a proportionate involvement within the surge of modelling activity.

To counter this loss, there has been a determined effort to attack more complex, less popular modelling problems and re-establish specialist skills such as manpower planning, although this remains minor activity attributed with limited involvement in the strategic decisions of most organisations. In practice corporate planning has provided a useful training ground for operational researchers to move upwards into more general business management, exposing the staff to fundamental higher levels of the business activity such as the assessment of a new venture rather than the details of production scheduling within that activity. Because of this lack of long term commitment to corporate planning and the reduced involvement, there has not been enough lateral thinking by operational researchers on different forms of modelling and at different levels of decision making.

Modelling for tactical analysis—resource application

Financial Modelling

Corporate modelling is dominated in practice by financial modelling, accounting for 90% of the activity. Hence the term corporate model is commonly used to describe a financial model which demonstrates the financial consequences over time of decisions with critical assumptions and within a close range of alternatives. The natural structure of financial reports lend themselves to a mechanical model format that allows the report to be generated repeatedly over time with different prime data.

There are two reasons why financial modelling can become a complex problem that merits the intervention of a specialist: (a) the size of the model/multiple components and (b) the sophistication of forecasts and relationships of elements in the model.

In the case of multiple "strategic business units" within an existing or planned investment, there is a need to handle and control the large quantity of data: to provide individual unit reports: and to design the mechanics of consolidated appraisal. The investment involved five strategic business units—crop farming, feedmilling, broiler meat production, egg production and central services. There were approximately five hundred individual data components. The units were structured to provide mutual benefits and joint economies. For example- crops were produced on the farm to provide feed for the laying hens—assessing the sensitivity of the results to market changes in the demand for eggs had to link back to the effect on the farm activity etc. as well as the planned flock sizes and laying cycles. In general there existed a complex lateral interaction of performance between units reflected in the model. Further the vertical impact of changes, for example in a capital cost, filtered through the capital schedule, the depreciation in the profit/loss accounts, the subsequent cash flow, draw down of loan requirement-compounded for interest charges etc.

The quality of the information out of any financial model is dependent on the ability of the model to represent reality. Whilst approximate estimates of revenues and cost can provide reasonable assessment, it may be necessary to include more accurate estimates incorporating sophisticated mathematical techniques. Costs may be projected using simple extrapolation or simple proportional relationships for simple results. The system has been derived by multivariate statistical analysis relations fuel consumption to the pattern of production activity and weather conditions.

The paper by Shim and McGlade provides a general "state of the art" summary of financial modelling, including both areas of the application-how models are used, and a description of the tools available—what computer packages are relevant. Modelling packages have developed over the last twelve years in two directions. Firstly, in the range of design, from the large data based main frame packages such as FCS to the micro spread-sheet packages such a VISICALC; secondly, in the quality of design in terms of facilities and use interface. From a survey of financial modelling in The Times 1000 companies, Grinyer has compiled a detailed statistical analysis of user experience in the construction and use of financial models. In contains a particularly useful investigation of experience with modelling packages-important for new practitioners. Bryant's edited collection of case histories gives a practical and detailed insight into financial modelling illustration a wide variety of applications.

Manpower Modelling

Finance is one resource to be considered in any tactical deployment to achieve a particular strategy. A second resource is that of manpower. Whilst manpower planning has not received the same level of attention as financial planning, there have been significant developments over the last ten years in bringing manpower modelling methods into the practical tool kit of corporate planners. Manpower is a considerably more complen issue than money. Its behaviour is subject to a multiplicity of factors and there are no simple measure of the effectiveness of its application. Developments have gone two ways: firstly more detailed stochastic models that attempt to reflect these additional factors and, secondly, simple modelling packages providing a limited but useful planning tool. Purkiss has summarised the state of the art with respect to the theory of manpower modelling systems. Edwards has described the packages commonly available. These models essentially comprise a system of stocks within classes and user defined rules for flows between classes. The use is limited by the treatment of aggregate behaviour and in most circumstances the same models can be constructed using financial planning packages, although there is undoubted benefit at the user interface from the prespecified manpower format. A common theme of successful applications is that good presentation of results and ease of use are more important to users than theoretical sophistication. Verhoeven discusses these tools as an aid to corporate planning and to the problems of designing alternative policies for promotions, recruitment, etc. through a case study. The application is a typical example of the successful use of models-namely where the profile of the organisation is consistent, there is an inherent rigid class/job description structure and where the stocks of similar personnel within classes are high enough to accept aggregate representation—in this case the Royal Dutch Airforce.

Resource Modelling

The models described above are perfect examples of decision support system—demonstrating the likely result from tactical planning decisions. The principle applies to planning of all resources. One of the most powerful decision support mechanisms for examining the application of resources is simulation. Craig describes the use of system dynamics; a simple simulation mechanism for corporate planning that incorporates non-financial resource, in this case material stocks and cash, using the package GENSIM. A more sophisticated model by Newton involves a discrete event colour graphic simulation system desired to play the resources at a new dock for grain export. The resources included grain storage capacity, weigh bridges, conveyor tracking, ship berth etc. -with interacting behaviour. The simulation enables the planners to predict the performance of the dock design with different schedules of grain carried and grain shipped out.

Simulation has two important contributions to planning:

1. demonstrating feasibility -predicting complex interactive behaviour and the ability of the resource to achieve the objectives
2. demonstrating risk -conveying the variability of performance and results.

However, in general, discrete event simulation requires specialist and complex modelling skill, a feature that reduces its applicability and acceptability in routine corporate planning practice. Although system dynamics may be a less powerful tool in predicting behaviour, it undoubtedly has had a larger exposure and application.

Strategic modelling

Tactical analysis accounts for 99% of the effort in model building within corporate planning and the consequent involvement of operational research. There remains however a significant deficiency of modelling tools for strategic decision making. There is a very important need for decision support system directed specifically at the top level policy making issues. Again there exists constant debati about how to define strategy. Johnson and Scholes group strategic decision into the following working descriptions:

sell out
consolidation
market penetration
product development
market development
diversification-related
-unrelated

and provide practical definitions of these options. Strategic modelling must attack the problem of supporting the decision mechanism for these options and predicting the likely "success" of the decision in meeting the organization's objectives.

Consider the original example. A group currenty active in the manufacture, distribution and export of animal feeds is now deciding whether to diversify, expanding its UK operation base by entering the pet food business. Question- "what decision support system will help to make that decision?" The contribution of modelling practice described within tactical analysis has limited value. A financial model projecting a potential acquisition would be questionable—its past data would relate to the existing management and provide little insight of future performance within the group. It is not easy to attempt to quantify the economies of synergy, operating the business within the group—market access, central management, material purchasing etc. The present financial prospectus for the business might provide a lower bound for the group's expectations but not much more. Further, the less tangible benefits of new distribution exposure for the existing business, and the long term opportunities based on the impending decision would be even more difficult to model and quantify. Frequently the error in constructing a detailed financial model with vast quantities of cost/revenue components with solid foundation provide a complex number crunching exercise with limited credibility. The traditional operational research philosophy of linking decisions to outcomes by a mechanical nuts and bolts building operation is not feasible.

At this stage it could be argned that entrepreneurial strategic decision making is an art, an inherent skill within the individual," gut feeling," with no room for objective analysis. Further it could be believed that only opportunities which are not mechanically obvious as good decisions allow for entrepreneurial flair - the successful horse race punter is the man who sees the chances of his horse winning higher than the general view as indicated by the betting odds. In the example, the chairman of the group might feel that it is "right" to make the pet foods acquisition. Indeed there are many successful small business owners who would accept this simple description of their strategic decision making.

A second theory of entrepreneurial behaviour that would rule out the value of strategic modelling is that of the lottery; that decision made on this haphazard approach are in fact a pure toos-of-the-coin gamble; and that some decisions are successful on a random basis. There is no doubt that the unknown outcome of decisions must contribute to the support of this theory and that there is a place for luck in the history of business success. However there is also a problem in tying this theory to examples of counting success and in general continuing survival of business organisations.

In practice, in this example, the group director identify and debate issues and aspects of the decision that have strategic significance-indicating potential success or failure from the outcome.

1. the group has considerable feed technology skills and experience related to pet feed manufacturing.
2. the group already manufacture and sell some of the base component suitable for pet feed
3. the existing distribution systems could be used to distribute pet food, including export business
4. the pet food market is a growth market particularly in new overseas economies
5. the group has surplus cash resources
6. some of the existing animal feed markets overseas are effectively in decline to traditional UK suppliers-exhibiting a similar profile to that of a conventional durable product life cycle
7. there is a minimal size of operation in the new

product area necessary to sustain the diversification as a success full business unit.

8. the cost of entering the main stream dog and cat food markets of the UK in terms of product promotion and pricing is very high.

The decision making process by the director involves a subconscious strategic modelling exercise with these and other factors as input and the likely results of the decision as output.

Although this is clearly a complex problem to approach, there have been some attempts to formalise this modelling and provide practical tools for corporate planners within limited circumstances.

Market Share Strategies

The PIMS study was initiated in 1971 by the American Marketing Science Institute and the Harvard Business School with the intention to examine the profit impact of market strategies through statistical analysis. The PIMS original data base comprised financial and other information on 620 individual businesses supplied by 57 major North American corporations initially for the three year period 1970-72. Since then the survey has been launched in the UK and continues as an important collection of business information. Buzzel, Gale and Sutton reported that PIMS project reveals a link between return on investment (ROI) and market share—"the bigger the better". They based this conclusion on the positive correlated observed between ROI and market share from the study data. The findings were supported by the three feasible explanations: economies of scale, market power, and quality of management. Further, the results suggested a predictable change in profit from an aggressive market building strategy.

The idea was enhanced by the Boston Consulting Group and their theory of the experience curve effect. They observed that "each time the accumulated experience of manufacturing a particular product doubles, the total unit cost in real terms... can be made to decline by a characteristic percentage", i.e. an increase in production volume results in a reduction of unit production cost.

Whilst there is considerable debate about the validity of these conclusions and concern for the statistical rigour of the interpretations they represent a new dimension in corporate modelling. This is the concept that the strategic decisions, as input, can be translated into the effect on profit, as output, through a systematic process. The PIMS finding, for example, implied that the direct consequences of a 5% increase in market share etc. could be predicted.

Portfolio Strategy

In the broader sense of modelling as a decision support system for corporate planning, there have been attempts to demonstrate the current development of resources and the likely results of strategy decisions through graphic systems. One common theme in corporate modelling is the need to present the decision makers with a critical summary of the large amount of potential data and analysis from a multi-business group. Several matrix representation techniques have been designed to provide a strategic map of resource deployment and a summary information image of existing and potential strategic. The first and most famous of these systems is the growth- share matrix of the Bostan Consulting Group Strategic business units are plotted on the matrix with two dimensions, business growth rate and market share. The matrix is divided into four strategic areas and units falling in those areas are designated with appropriate titles and descriptions. The projected movement from one quadrant to the next indicate the weaknesses in the group structure; the required strategy and the anticipated outcome of that strategy. Whilst again there remains argument about the validity of the inherent analysis, the contribution to corporate modelling is very important. Firstly it provides a new line of thought on information representation for strategic decision making and secondary it shows an attempt to advance the one factor model into a two factor model for predicting the decision outcome.

This represent an attempt to model the input of five different factor and the strategic decision from those factors on the implied outcome profit etc. As a decision support system the procedure demonstrates the critical information about the present portfolio of business and the likely outcome from decisions on diverification through acquisition; sell out; market share building; etc.

These matrix system have two futures:

(a) they can only handle the modelling of two factors at any onetype

(b) they are designed for simple accounting factors

Qualitative issues

Robinson, Hichens and Wade have extended the growth share matrix to include a border range of qualitative factor in assessing the strategic disposition of the organization's business units and those of its competitors with the Directional Policy Matrix. They have expanded market growth to "business sector prospects"-a general measure of the health of the industry, and market share to " company's competitive capabilities"-a general measure of the business unit's relative competitiveness within that industry. The measures are determined by accumulating the simple subjective scores to a series of prescribed questions for each factor. The questions are concerned with qualitative strategic issues rather than quantitative financial analysis. The resulting two-score answer can then be plotted on a two dimensional matrix divided into nine strategic areas and the positions interpreted to assist the planning process.

The tool was further extended by Hussey to include a third factor, environmental risk—a measure of the stability of the external circumstances that directly affect the industry.

Newton showed that the same system, with a rearrangement of priorities and weighting of individual factors, could be used to approach potential acquisitions.

The Directional Policy Matrix and its derivatives require three basic assumptions:

(a) that all qualitative issues can be assessed in quantitative terms

(b) that all the issues can be clustered into three fundamental dimensions

(c) that the relative significance of different issues within the same dimension can be reflected by a weighted summation process.

McNamee provides a detailed description and comparison of these and other matrix display techniques-how the choice of matrix to be used by strategic planners is dependent on the objectives of the exercise and the data available. The common theme behind matrix methods is a decision support system that interprets the current disposition of resources in a concise display in an attempt to point to obvious strategic decisions, and their likely affect on achieving the organisation's objectives.

Corporate planning and operational research–the future

Harris devised the sphere of corporate planning problems into four sectors defined by two dimensions, (a) the degree of understanding of actions and their effects, (b) the degree of change from the existing practice. The paper suggests that

Operational Research can make significant contributions in the three sectors. In the spectrum of decisions within the corporate planning process, problems with these profiles typically fall within the areas of tactical analysis whilst strategic decisions involve high change and, at present, low understanding.

The contribution of corporate modelling for resource allocation within tactical analysis will continue to provide a powerful tool for planners. The development in corporate modelling popularity should prompt future interest in more sophisticated systems with more complex modelling mechanisms driven by larger and more varied data bases, and hence a future role for "bread and butter" operational research. Little has been done to link sophisticated forecasting techniques to modelling procedures. There are serious problems in "controlling" model use, ensuring the data is correct, protecting the logic mechanism and the user!

To encourage the interest and ensure the operational research contribution, the inconvenience of having a specialist between the model and the decision makers needs to be overcome. It is imperative therefore that operational researchers have a good education in business principles. Accounting should have the same level of significance in the skills of operational researchers as the more established disciplines such as statistics. Operational research should be examining the process of information presentation to the decision maker, a feature that has been helped by the fact that decision support as well as decision optimisation has been recognised as part of the "approved" subject material.

Modelling for strategic decision making, the quadrant provides the greatest challenge to operational researchers. Taking our example a stage further, the animal feed group has now found a potential acquisition, a small family business currently supplying about 30% (£1.5 M) of a segment within the pet food market. The company has an existing distribution network supplying about 100 wholesalers throughout the UK and is earning a small profit.

Can operational research provide a mechanism to translate these complex interrelated qualitative factors into a decision support system that predicts the consequences of the alternate decisions?

Some issues are not unique to corporate planning. The problems of handling multiple qualitative factors is common to the general development of multi-criteria decision analysis. Such mechanisms as Saaty's eigenvector technique for combining multiple qualitative factors is one possible tack to consider. Extending the current matrix methods into more complex strategic maps that allow the presentation of a more complex resource image for portfolio and competitor analysis provides a challenge to operational researchers to stretch their information technology skills and imagination. It has already been suggested that the developments in expert systems could close the gap in the loop between resource allocation and its strategic implications. " The possibility is clear that within a decade a supercomputer may share or usurp functions of a corporate chief executive-functions that up to now have been thought unsharable. Now is the item to begin planning for such a development."

In general if operational research is to regain a significant role in corporate planning and the evolution of its theory, it must think beyond existing boundaries of the formal and established practices. It must also be prepared to take risk and fall on its nose from time to time to demonstrate its willingness to consider "weak" contributions and divergent thinking. Whilst the potential contribution to these "wicked problems" remains unsure, there is a very big hole and a demand that is ready to welcome that contribution.

6 Optimisation in Manufacturing, Marketing and Control

Determination of the optimum manufacturing plan, based on requirements forecasting, involves a careful appraisal of many cost variables. The fundamental problem is to develop a production schedule that will utilize men, machinery, and materials most effectively in meeting requirements. In addition, the manufacturing area presents the most complex information and control problem in many companies. The failure to integrate the applicable techniques into the information flow system has often resulted in continuous panic situations.

Our treatment in this book deals with optimization of the manufacturing process as such, primarily in terms of the most effective planning, scheduling, and production of products. The assumption is made that optimum advantage has already been taken of specific measures to improve efficiency, such as setting of standards, use of incentives, reduction of scrap, control of maintenance, replacement of equipment, control of personnel, and other such standard measures.

Development of an optimum manufacturing plan must take into consideration the relative costs and advantages of longer runs and fewer setups, versus shorter runs and more frequent setups—as far as a particular product or part is concerned. This means balancing the costs of holding inventories against the costs of manufacturing a smaller lot size more frequently. At the same time, provision has to be made for lead time and safety stock to be sure that stockouts do not occur too frequently. The problem would be relatively simple if only a few products were being manufactured, but unfortunately, in most cases many different products or parts are being made. The objective in such cases is one of utilizing the various resources available in labour and plants to produce the items on time and at the minimum cost. It becomes necessary to schedule various products through the plant in such a way that balance is maintained between various departments, so that men and machines in different departments are kept busy, and at the same time inventory at various production centres does not accumulate byond control.

It is apparent that the lead time is affected by the in-process inventory on hand and by the manufacturing mix, as well as by the characteristics of the product itself. Therefore, optimizing in manufacturing involves more than simply optimizing for each individual product. The plan should provide information in advance as to detailed work loads and proper scheduling to optimize the end result.

Production and materials planning

Perhaps the place to start in development of the most effective production plan is by the analysis of products or parts which must be manufactured. Which products will require the most manufacturing time, how often must they be manufactured, and in what quantity? Probably some items will be manufactured on a regular basis, others only infrequently. Naturally the type of company has a dominant effect on this problem. If basis, obviously its problem is completely different from one which manufactures thousands of individual small tools.

ABC Classification

It is important for manufacturing to separate the important few items from the less important many for appropriate controls and for requency and detail of reporting. Here again, we expect the typical distribution—a small percentage of items usually represents a high percentage of dollar activity.

The most effective way to classify parts is, first, to multiply the annual usage by the direct manufacturing cost per unit; the total annual items costs can then be ranked in order of magnitude and the classifications assigned. When such data are already available in the cost system and, especially, if they are on punched cards, the classification can be carried out in a very short time.

Once this has been accomplished, a distribution curve can be plotted that should suggest approximate division points between A, B, and C categories. Having determined this separation, the ABC concept should now be exploited to the fullest extent. Special attention may have to be given to the expensive but infrequently used items that may not fall into the A category under the above classification system.

The A items will normally have smaller EOQs (in months of supply) and be cycled more frequently. The should have lower reorder points because this reduction usually more than offsets the cost of expediting. These items should be reviewed for reduction in materials, setup, and cycle costs, because a small percentage of saving usually has a larger dollar effect with this category of item. These parts should be scheduled most accurately in order to reduce work-in-process inventory; wherever possible, their stock should be depleted before they are made obsolete. The materials handling plan should be developed to provide the best service for the A category.

At the other extreme, C items will normally have relatively large EOQs. They should have high reorder points so that they do not require close and costly control. In fact, they often can be handled by group posting, or by the "last container" method of reordering. C items can sometimes be categorized for EOQ computation, rather that being handled individually. B items fall in between these two extremes for treatment.

Some of the typical approaches suggested for ABC analysis are as follows:

1. Items with similar setup characteristics should be grouped together.
2. Interchangeable items should be grouped before solving for the EOQ value.
3. Specific raw materials should be directly incorporated into manufacturing costs.
4. General raw materials should be included in manufacturing EOQ computations only if such decisions change the purchasing practices. Where the level of such inventories is more affected by price breaks than by EOQ, the raw material should be left out of the manufacturing EOQ decision rule.

Economic lot sizes

Most products are manufactured in lots or batches. The principal exceptions are in the processing field, where products are made on a continuous flow basis, or for various mass-produced consumer products where a production line for a product may run continuously. The problems involved in optimizing for non-lot-type products will be discussed later. "At this point , however, we wish to discuss the least cost manufacture of lot-type products.

For a lot-type product there are three main considerations: (1) How many units should be manufactured in a lot or batch, i.e. the economic lot size? (2) How low can the quantity on hand be permitted to drop before placing a production order? (3) How much stock must be on hand at the time of reordering to provide protection against variations from normal demand? This safety stock may represent protection against random fluctuations in demand or it may represent "interposition waiting " needed for known seasonal variations from average.

The factors involved in determination of the economic lot size, the reorder point, and the safety stock are all different, but related.

Lot-size inventories. The lot size portion of inventory reaches a maximum upon receipt of a new order and on the average is fully exhausted just before the arrival of the next order. Although the depletion is usually irregulal, the assumption that it takes place on a linear basis has worked satisfactorily in almost every situation. Consequently, the average level of a lot-size and inventory is half the lot size. Under economic order quantity control, the lot size and inventory level becomes a reasonably stable situation, responding primarily to trends in usage.

Safety inventories. Safety inventories give a cushion against normal fluctuations in demand and supply. These functuations are unpredictable. They are expected to occur in a randon manner and have no correlation with season of the year or other identified factors. Although difficult to rate in dollars, stock outs represent true cost and justify the expense of a calculable safety inventory.

The amount of safety stock is affected by the protection desired against stockouts, the variability of demand and supply, and the protection already achieved from the lot size portion of the inventory.

Anticipation Inventories: Anticipation inventories cover predicted changes in demand and the corresponding adjustment in inventory. These inventories may be built to cover introduction of new products, changes in distribution methods or any known factor that will affect supply and demand. Anticipation will reduce employment fluctuations, overtime costs, and the need for reserve capacity in cyclical industries. In some cases, computer simulation programs can aid in planning the amount and timing of anticipation inventories.

EOQ Theory. In applying optimizing techniques, manufacturing must determine economic manufacturing quantities. The mathematical relationships to be used here differ from those used in procurement in that they include the cost of setups, as well as processing of shop orders.

Although EOQ is now recognized as the greatest single contribution to industrial operations research, the concept did not receive immediate acceptance. At first, there was a lack of education and understanding, which lasted for a period of 20 to 30 years prior to 1945; the next problem was the lack of good data, i.e., no setup or order costs; third, in the period around 1955, there were many questions about the "value of money."

The EOQ is at the point where the cost of acquisition of inventory equals the cost of carrying inventory. These costs vary with the size of the lot. Because of this, any movement from the point where they are equal will increase the total variable costs.

The setup costs are the out-of-pocket costs that would not be incurred if a setup were eliminated. They include the time for the setup plus other expenses by shortened runs, such as increased chance for human or mechanical failure.

Inventory carrying charges represent expenses in storage costs, obsolescence, taxes, and insurance, and—most important—the value of money. Both manual and data processing methods are available for calculation of new EOQs or EOQ revisions, based on changes of any of the variables in the formula.

The calculation of the EOQ formula for each product can be facilitated by the use of nomographs, or, if the numbers are very large, by the use of a computer.

Electronic Data Processing of EOQs: While nomographs can facilitate manual processing of EOQ calculations, it will be obvious that many situations lend themselves to the use of mechanical and electronic processing. Punch-card equipment and computers may perform the operations shown on either or both of the nomographs.

As an illustration, in one application punch-card processing made the initial K calculations for all parts. This information was then stored in computer memory, where it was regularly combined with the latest usage information for EOQ calculation. Occasionally, some parts required recalculation of K, which was done by nomograph. When the company added a large number of new items to the line, punch-card calculation again was most economical.

EOQs for Assembly Lots: Where the assembly cycle is very short compared to the lead time for component part production, economic order quantities should not be calculated individually for each component, unless the components are used in several different assemblies. One electronics manufacturer discovered this shortly after applying EOQs, when he ran out of the major component whose EOQ was only 50, after 50 assemblies of a planned lot of 200. He had to wait five weeks to get a special order of the remaining 150.

A similar situation can happen when the assemblies are going to be built in lots or batches with substantial time gaps between orders. A manufacturer of portable electric generators had this type of activity. It was important to have all units for the assembly run at the outset and no inventory except for spares between assembly lots.

Frequently, companies using EOQ rule resolve these by dilemmas increasing safety stocks, which is an expensive and unnecessary solution.

The manufacturer of assembly lots can be resolved on an EOQ plan by totalling the setup and unit costs of the specific components as opposed to components used on several assemblies. This summary should include assembly setup costs, but exclude the setup on parts common to other assemblies. These summarized figures can be used in the conventional lEOQ formula to determine the lot size for the assembly. Any component with a specific EOQ lower than the assembly value should have its EOQ raised to this value.

Value of money: The value placed by management upon money is a critical element in the analysis of manufacturing costs, as well as in the analysis of procurement and distribution costs yet to be discussed. There will probably be as many different ideas about the value to be placed on money as there are companies.

In any initial installation, it is well to sample to existing decision rules before selecting the value of money invested in inventory. For example, if a statistically weighted average of existing rules places the value of money invested in inventory at approximately 35 per cent, and without realizing this, management decides to optimize inventories by balancing with a cost of, say, 6 per cent, the resulting buildup in inventory would be so drastic that it would create considerable embarrassment. This might well discredit the attempt to establish optimum decision rules, in the light of post practices.

On the other hand companies might select a relatively high value for money invested in inventory—say, 30 per cent without realizing that the decision rules historically in effect are equivalent to placing the value of money at 10 per cent. The resulting saving in inventory might look attractive, but a substantial jump in costs might result from greatly increased setup and order-writing expense compared to past performance.

The average value of money as reflected in current order quantity decision rules provides a good starting point in an optimizing program. When this average value is applied in the formula for all parts individually, a reduction in total investment in inventory as well as reductions in actual setup and order costs, will result. Although this two-way cost reduction may seem paradoxical. The explanation is of course, that the company was ordering low value goods too frequently, and and high-value goods not frequently enough.

By such a calculation, with an appropriate sample, management can be shown how a policy decision either increasing or decreasing the value of money will affect the optimum inventory level. The calculation also shows what it costs to depart from this level.

It is important to note that management is at liberty to change its stipulated value of money. The new value can be used in the appropriate formulas, and new levels of inventory can be determined to reflect changes desired in return on investment. For example, the financial officer of a company believed to be entering a recession may raise the value for total carrying charges in the decision rule in order to obtain the desired amount of inventory liquidation. This decision would reflect his conviction that the risk of excess money in inventory and obsolescence is greater than investing the money elsewhere. A year later, when confidence returns, he may change to a value even lower that the original, because an investment in the company's own inventory at that time and rate may be the soundest decision that he can make. The important point about these optimizing rules is that where the formula is applied in place of a straight-time reorder system or an exact component balance stock system, there is a potential reduction in inventory of 15 to 25 per cent, and a commensurate potential reduction of 15 to 25 per cent in setup and changeover casts.

Protection against shortages

Lead Times: The number of units that should be manufactured in a lot or batch is determined by the EOQ formula. The amount of inventory of a part that should be on hand when the production order is placed will depend on the lead time, i.e., the time that will elapse between the placing of the order and getting the finished product into inventory. Enough inventory must be kept on hand to meet normal demands during this period. This quantity is in addition to the safety stock that is maintained to meet abnormal demand requirements.

It is vitally important, therefore, to determine

the lead time per unit product or part, and at the same time to analyze the lead time variations. In many complex manufacturing situations, there are unnecessarily long lead times in the decision rules used for production planning. Methods of analyzing lead times and reasonable work-in-process inventory levels are discussed later in the chapter.

Safety Stocks: Safety stock is defined as the amount of stock required to cover variations in demand during the lead time period and variations in the lead time itself. The reorder point is determined by adding the average usage during the lead time to the safety stock. Thus, if there were no variation on usage or lead time, the safety stock could be zero and the reorder point would be so determined that the last unit would be issued as the new supply became available.

The amount of safety stock required for any product or part is determined from an analysis of the lead time and usage. It is not sufficient, however, in calculation either the lead time or the usage to work with simple average figures. For a system to work effectively, it is necessary to consider variation around the averages as well as the interrelationship of one person with another. A variety of statistical techniques are used, therefore, to provide figures that will give good results not only under average conditions, but also under conditions with considerable spread from the average.

The relationship between stockouts protection

and EOQ inventory also needs clarification. In the calculation of safety stocks, the amount of time covered by one economic order quantity must be considered. For the same level of protection, an item that is ordered in lots of one year's usage need less safety stock than an item that is reordered once a month.

Use of statistical techniques in safety stock and reorder point calculations

The use of the various techniques for determining reorder points and safety stocks can best be illustrated by a fairly detailed step-by-step description of a specific situation. In the following example, which is adopted from our application in a client's plant, thousands of parts are manufactured and assembled into a number of different complex units. Parts are controlled through the ordering of assemblies.

Two basic ways of using sampling and variation analysis will concern us. One is to determine the variations in usage or lead time, etc.,for a particular part; the other is to determine variation in lead time, or usage, etc., for a group of parts based on a sample. In some cases it will not be worth the effort required to obtain data on each part, and figures based on a representative sample will be adequate.

In the following discussion we consider the methods of determining the usage variation, purchasing lead time variations, and manufacturing lead time variations.

In this case, since many thousands of parts were involved, sampling was used to determine the expected variations from averages. The method of sampling and the manner in which the sample results were applied will be described. Because there are interactions between variations in each element, the safety stocks are not calculated until the variation for each element is known.

The standard deviations of monthly usage were then expressed as a percentage of average monthly usage for each item in the sample. A mean of the averages of the parts in A, B and C groups was then obtained. There was then an average standard deviation for A parts, another for B parts, and a third for C parts.

The amount of safety stock required for each part to protect against usage variation could then be determined by computing the average monthly usage for each part and multiplying it by the appropriate average standard deviation percentage. Thus, if the monthly usage of a particular A part was 200, and the average standard deviation percentage obtained from the sample of A parts was 150 per cent, the safety stock required to provide protection against usage variations would be 300 units at 97.5 per cent confidence limits.

If the usage variation were the only one which concerned us, this figure would be correct. Because of interactions among variations in usage, purchased lead time, and manufacturing lead time, the total safety stock is not the sum of the safety stocks calculated separately, but rather can be determined only by considering these interactions as will be shown after the section on manufacturing lead time variation.

Purchasing Lead Time Variation. The purchasing lead time variation was determined in a manner similar to that used for usage variation. A sample of purchased parts was drawn, stratified, and grouped according to type of material or part purchased. Posting sheets were used for the computations as follows:

1. Post requisition date and receiving date for past three purchase orders for a given item.
2. Subtract requisition date from receiving date to determine lead time for each order. Compare average lead time.
3. Subtract average lead time from actual lead time for each order, and post the difference or variation.
4. Total variations, regardless of size. and compute average variation.
5. Multiply average variation by 1.25 to get standard deviation of purchasing lead time.

The standard deviation for each item was then expressed as a percentage of the average lead time for the item, and for each group of purchased items the mean of these standard deviations was obtained.

Manufacturing Lead Time Variation: The

manufacturing lead time variation was also based on a selected sample. The procedure was as follows:

1. Select a sample of approximately 30 to 40 parts and obtain copies of their routings.
2. Prepare posting sheets, listing each part and showing all operations and departments involved. Provide space for posting two lots of each part, and for posting times clocked in and out of each operation.
3. Select two lots of each part processed during a recent, fairly stable period, and from time tickets, post actual dates clocked in and out of each operation.
4. Subtract dates out of each operation from dates into the following operation and post these historical external move times in days.
5. Where more than one operation is performed on a part, average internal move times within the department can be determined by subtracting total process time from total time in the department and dividing by 1 less than the number of operations. This can be done on a sampling basis.
6. Standard deviations of lead time are computed directly from average move time standard deviations as follows:
   a. Determine the number of departments through which the average part move.
   b. Compute one manufacturing lead time

standard deviation as the square root of the sum of the squares of all external and internal move time deviations.

$$\sigma ML = \sqrt{\text{number operations} \times \Sigma (\sigma M)^2}$$

Safety Stock Computations: Having determined on the basis of samples the standard deviation for A, B and C items in usage, purchasing lead time, and manufacturing lead time, it was possible to obtain the safety stock required to protect against variations in all three elements. Log scale nomographs which combine usage variation histograms with replenishment variation histograms into a safety stock histogram can be constructed to cover the safety stock variation.

As indicated earlier, the safety stock is not merely the sum of the quantities required for protection against usage, purchasing lead time, and manufacturing lead time, but rather depends on the interaction of these various elements. Calculations of the safety stock are based.

The important point to note is that for each of the thousands of parts, the average monthly usage and purchasing lead time are calculated; the standard deviations in usage and purchasing lead time are taken from the sample. The manufacturing lead time is based on average move time for various types of products, depending on the number of operations involved; the manufacturing lead time standard deviation is obtained from the sample.

The safety stocks finally determined should be modified for the lot-size effect mentioned earlier.

In the discussion above we described a system for determining safety stocks which depends on sampling at different stages in the calculation. The extent to which sampling can be used effectively will depend on the number of parts involved and the nature of the manufacturing operation.

The total lead time variation on an order can be determined by an overall plot of the elapsed time from start to finish by individual parts or categories similar to the method. Frequently, however, this is not accurate enough for production scheduling, as discussed later in this chapter.

Safety Stocks Related to Unfilled Orders. There has been some confusion in inventory control literature as to the meaning of the "protection" obtained at the 1, 2 and 3 sigma levels. Most of the formulas in current us actually indicate protection in terms of the number of zero balances rather than in stockout risk.

1σ = 16% risk of zero balance
2σ = 2.3% risk of zero balance
3σ = .15% risk of zero balance

$$\text{Sigma level} = \frac{\text{number of items at zero balance}}{\text{total number of active items}}$$

The actual stockouts will be influenced by the number of items demanded during the length of the stockout;

Per cent stockout = number of items demanded but unfilled/total of all items demanded

This percentage will be substantially higher than suggested by the number of zero balances, because the number of unfilled orders will reflect repeat demands, while the total number of items ordered in any period is usually less than the total number of active items.

A more useful indicator is the calculation of the "expected per cent of unfilled orders."

$$\frac{\text{Per cent zero balances} \times \text{average days duration} \times \text{average orders/day/}}{\text{Total orders during period}}$$

The actual performance against this measure can be computed easily, but it requires careful statistical work to plan safety stocks to arrive at the desired level.

A final measure of performance can be

$$\frac{\text{Dollars of delayed or lost sales}}{\text{Total dollars sold plus dollars lost}}$$

This is very meaningful because the dollars in the numerator can be converted to risk level or lost profits and compared to the extra inventory investment required to carry a higher level of protection.

Reorder Point Calculation: Reorder point is equal to the safety stock previously discussed plus the average usage during the average lead time.

The following paragraphs cover a slightly

different method of arriving at safety stocks, including an anticipation factor.

Optimum RPs derive from a consideration of variability in usage and lead time and the risk of zero stock balances management desires.

The anticipation factor may be calculated or included on the basis of management judgment. If a special advertising campaign is planned, the amount of anticipation may be determined by reference to past experience. Where seasonal data are available or price increases are anticipated, the amount of anticipation may be calculated by the formula.

Order Frequency: Order frequency does have an important effect on the timing of the update in of EOQs and reorder points. A review in one company indicated that some items had as much activity each month as others did each quarter, six months, or year. These items were approximately categorized into one-, three-, six-, twelve-month review periods. Updating inactive items on a monthly basis does not have statistical validity. Furthermore, if zero sales occurred for several months, the updating and smoothing formulas would predict the future incorrectly. The following section on updating recognizes the order frequency problem.

Updating formulas

The preceding discussion has indicated the methods used to calculate EOQs, reorder points, lead times, and safety stock. In any application of these techniques the most important task, after the initial calculations are made, is to keep the system operating effectively under changing conditions of demand for the various products.

It will be noted that, once an original EOQ is established, it varies directly with * U_M. Likewise, RP varies directly with U_M. Actual usages will vary in a random fashion from period to period. Frequently, they will also vary in a discernible trend. The system response should not jump EOQs and RPs up and down with every random variations but should spot trends as rapidly as possible.

With some control plans, no changes will be made in production plans unless control limits are exceeded. In other cases, some type of tracking method will be used and forecasts will be updated continuously. For example, an exponential smoothing formula with second-order factors to spot trends may be used.

A special computer program can be used to make predictions and to update U_M and thus EOQ and RP. This formula not only projects on the basis of historical averages but also followed trends in usage. In actual computer operation, this formula is converted to updating factors K and K^2 which operate directly on EOQ, RP and U_M.

Updating for each item should take place at an interval dependent on order frequency—the less frequent the orders, the longer the history period necessary for valid predictions. Specifically, items might be up—dated at intervals of either 1,

3, 6 or 12 months. Another special computer program would review each item from time to time to be sure it is in the proper updating category-class 1,3,6 or 12.

In the preceding sections we have described some of the calculations required to determine EOQs, safety stock, lead times, and recorder points. In the following example, a complete inventory control system is described to illustrate how these various techniques fit into the control operation.

In many manufacturing situations the parts or products operate independently of each other and can be controlled by the program. This control program assumes that the demands for each item will reduce the available stock below the reorder point and that the EOQ will be triggared when this occurs. This is known as forward scheduling because all activities work forward from the date the reorder point is reached.

In the inventory control system described below, many components of a few complex machines are involved. We are concerned, therefore, with the problem of completing many related activities on a specific date. Failure to complete any one of these activities may seriously delay the entire assembly. Therefore, we design the system to anticipate the total demands created by the forecast of the assembly. Because of the long lead times involved for certain components, it is necessary to work backward from the forecasted assembly date to the date for issuing the order for each component.

In this specific plan, the forecast quantity is then exploded into sub-assembly and component demands by RAMAC.

Based upon the bills of material decks and the lead times and reorder points, RAMAC reserves each assembly and, subsequently, components, if the assembly is below the reorder point. If the reservation reduces the available below the reorder point, an advance reservation card is issued. Except for the longest leads time, the advance reservation cards are filed in a suspense deck by pull-out dates, which will start them on their way in time to make the final due date. The advance reservation deck also provides an opportunity for simulation and release of work ahead of time to level out shop loads.

When the pull-out date arrives, the advance reservation cards are reprocessed through RAMAC to see if the order is still required and to net, write purchase and shop orders, etc.

When raw material is required, a raw material requisition and purchase order, if required, may also be triggered. Where subassemblies are involved, it is necessary to round EOQs to multiples of the subsumable quantity.

The input data are collected in one or more data cards for transmission into RAMAC. These data become the semipermanent control data upon which the inventory control program functions. The string analysis is the modification of EOQs by subassembly or common usage characteristics that have been previously discussed. The usage upon which the reorder points and EOQs depend is developed in the lower left where forecasts, parts list, and usage posting are merged and analyzed to supply average usage (U_M) and usage deviation (σU_M). Proceeding up the left-hand side, the development of setup and component unit costs leads to ABC value usage analysis and EOQ calculations. Proceeding up the right-hand side, the lead time (L_M) and lead time deviation (σM_L) are developed for purchasing and manufacturing and form the basic data for safety stock and reorder point calculations. The EOQs are modified for discount and price-break calculations in the upper right.

Continuous flow inventories

Continuous flow inventories are typified by the gas pipeline network in many parts of the country. The volume through the lines, or the number of lines in service, represents an inventory function. In other situations, there is a lot depletion and replenishment cycle, but it is so rapid that it has the characteristics of the continuous flow process and can be treated in this fashion if the start-up, shut-down or changeover costs are not significant.

The continuous process inventory problem raises the following questions as to service and optimization:

1. Is there sufficient inventory at the service point to cover variations in demand?
2. Where the above method is not feasible, is there sufficient standby potential to feed demand?

3. If the production alternatives offer different costs, what combinations provide the least costly answer?

In the following section on production control a linear programming case study will be discussed. The safety stock problem with continuous flow lends itself to the concepts already presented.

Production control

Production control varies more in techniques and importance over a border span than any other control function in industry. In companies that produce relatively few items with relatively few operations in a single plant, the whole function can be accomplished as a part-time job by the factory manager or his assistant. As the number of items, operations, or plants begin to multiply, the problems quickly go beyond the scope of human imagination. A complex job shop with 20,000 components, with 10 operations each in 30 potential work centers, could well require years of running on a large-scale computer to be absolutely sure that the schedule was optimum. Fortunately, in these complex situations the exact answer isn't that much of an improvement over a reasonably good schedule. But even a reasonably good schedule in complex situations has had to await EDP capabilities before it was readily attainable.

In the area of production control, the following types of problems must have continual solution:

1. What has to be accomplished within each time period?

2. What sequences of assignment is most likely to give the optimum answer in meeting total schedule dates?
3. What is the best amount of work-in-process inventory or "float" to balance idle-time costs against cost of carrying inventory?
4. As conditions change from forecast, what items can be advanced and retarded to give the best utilization of manpower and facilities to meet objectives?
5. Of the alternatives available, which assignment will provide the lowest cost?

The preceding discussion of inventory control and its relation to production planning has shown various considerations that must be taken into account to determine what items should be manufactured, at what times, and in what quantities. These initial decisions may in part have to be altered somewhat when the actual production schedules are prepared. The production orders that result from the analysis discussed so far in this chapter must be scheduled in a way that will permit the most effective and lowest cost use of facilities, without drastically altering the lead times and order quantities indicated by the individual EOQ calculations.

After production has been scheduled on a controlled basis for a period, it will probably be well to resample lead times, because they may have changed significantly as a result of the better control plan. The interrelationships between optimization of individual product requirements and optimization of production of all items must be continually kept in mind in order to obtain the best results.

Before discussing the preparation of work load reports and queue lists we will discuss some of the analytical work required in the preparation of the basic data for such reports.

Work-in-process analysis

Work-loading and queuing formulas frequently involve an analysis of service channels or machines available for various operations, since the amount of float time and, hence, inventory required per machine, goes down as the number of available service channels goes up.

It is easy for an engineer to recognise insufficient work in process if he can see that workers have idle time during the day. He can also easily recognise when the plant is loaded with work in process far beyond the needs of flexibility, because of the in-plant transportation problems created. Unfortunately, the majority of cases are somewhere between these two extremes, and statistical analysis is required to determine the proper scheduling to optimize work in process.

A statistical sampling over a period of weeks or months can be made, covering the variation of work-in-process inventory available to each work center. From not more than 10 to 15 readings at each location, it is possible to project statistically the variation characteristics of work in process, even in extremely complex department-to-department work flows. By comparing the lowest projection of work in process just ahead of each work center with the maximum potential of that center to *produce* work in a given period, it is possible to calculate whether the work in process is excessive, just right, or insufficient. Where it is insufficient, the lead time should be increased; where excessive, it should be lowered.

For example: if our sample indicated that the amount of work available at a specific work center for 15 successive weeks was:

500 hours	700	1,000
800	800	800
600	500	700
700	400	900
900	600	600

Lowest = 400 hours
Median = 700 hours

Work-center Load Reports: The computer can add into the load of each work center the additional total hours of all jobs released including the lead time adjustment for the specific center. It can also subtract out the equivalent hours when the operation is completed.

The computer can store detail operation loading information and produce schedules from these data. Where necessary to reduce bottlenecks or facilitate rework, economic lots can be split, and rescheduled, and loads adjusted accordingly. Scrap losses should be debited against inventory and should not produce replacement orders unless they drop the available balance below the reorder point.

Queue Lists. The computer can produce reports of all jobs in the waiting line, or queue, at each work center. The hours of work can be listed for each specific job, and extended and totalled for the complete queue. The computer can issue required dates for each work center on queue lists. New queue lists can be issued every day, and the new dates should override those previously issued. It may be desirable to issue the reports every other day or to list only those jobs due in the current week, with complete reporting on a periodic basis, in order to keep the lists less voluminous.

Control of dates by queue lists permits jobs to be rescheduled by unloading outstanding operations and reloading corrected figures without changing paper work in the plant. Jobs can be queued by the date and location of the lowest unfinished operation number, whether or not jobs are run in sequence. Rework jobs can be rescheduled for prior queues and related as necessary to facilitate completion on schedule.

A comparison of the scheduled work-center Load and actual qucuc load at each work center can be made to indicate bottlenecks and potential idle areas. Queue lists can be used to determined short-range requirements involving overtime or redistribution of the work force, and can also be used to locate parts in process and to revise production plans.

Jobs which are running slightly ahead of wanted dates should be considered on schedule. Safety stocks have been provided for lead time and usage variation. Jobs which are running more significantly behind schedule should appear on weekly past-due lists and may require expediting.

An advance reservation or demand card reduces the available stock below the reorder point. Shop orders, time cards, and move tickets are automatically created. The operation card deck is loaded into a memory track and the program calculates the hours required for each operation.

Work-load reports produced by the computer will show the total man-hour requirements for each work center for all shop orders. These work loads will be projected on the basis of lead time factors and accumulated in the appropriate week for the specific center involved. The work-load detail will be carried in memory so that reports can be adjusted for all important changes. Manufacturing supervision should plan manpower requirements, transfers, and overtime on these reports as modified by the more current information on the queue lists.

RAMAC will issue queue lists that show jobs in the sequence of data wanted at each work center. These lists will be used to provide all the date-due information for manufacturing supervision. The lists will show performance against schedule and indicate the areas requiring immediate corrective action. RAMAC will issue weekly past-due reports for control purposes, listing only job requiring special attention.

RAMAC will supply the material issue cards extended by the required quantities to cover stock withdrawals for the assembly floor. These cards will be used for updating the stock position and for cost purposes.

Engineering change procedures will be modified to control changes on a random EOQ release instead of a project-release basis. Engineering will establish when the change is to become effective and the disposition of obsolete parts. Inventory control will make necessary part and assembly number changes, and feed back to engineering a record of the completed change, identified by serial number of the first machine affected.

When the job arrives in stock the inventory availability is updated.

The stock room should keep records of physical stock on hand with the actual in-and-out transactions in each case. These can be central records or bin records, or a combination. The control of obligated stock will be the responsibility of RAMAC and, where necessary, the situation in relation to a particular assembly program can be printed out.

Stock room pickups will be made using the punched cards supplied by RAMAC. The pickups become the responsibility of the appropriate assembly foreman on issue.

It may be advisable to permit breaking in on an active operation where advancing the due date to the top of every queue list is not sufficiently rapid. Such jobs should also have special notation on the queue lists that are issued by RAMAC.

RAMAC should provide a program for a control report on per cent success in meeting due dates for each work center. This would give production control and manufacturing management a measurement of the effectiveness of the production foremen is carrying out total planning.

The specific formula for per cent success is as follows:

$$\frac{\text{Jobs completed ahead or on schedule}}{\text{total jobs completed}}$$

In order not to penalize the foremen who received jobs late, the numerator of this expression should be modified to include late jobs that were processed within the normal period after arrival.

Critical Ratio Method of Queuing and Work Loading

In recent applications of computer systems to complex job-shop situations, we have been experimenting with a critical ratio method of control. This ratio is designed to respond to feedback from the time the manufacturing order is written until it is received in stock or in the distribution area.

Safety stocks are provided as described in earlier sections to protect against variations in average usage or lead times during the replenishment time. Without safety stocks and with reorder points established on average usage and average lead time, half of the orders will arrive ahead of the stockout conditions and half of them after that time. In the first case, either lower demand or less lead time has combined to have a favourable effect; in the latter, high demand or lead time has caused the potential stockout.

Where the lead time is long or the variations from the average are large, use of the approach described below presents an opportunity to compensate for actual variations that take place in usage during the replenishment period by corresponding counter adjustments in the speed at which the order moves through production. Thus, if usage is higher than anticipated during the replenishment time, the lead time may be shortened by expenditing items through manufacturing. The key to the success of this operation is rapid feedback of actual data to the system.

Depending upon the company, its operations, and relationships of usage to lead time, it may be possible to eliminate safety stock entirely or to cut down on the degree of protection provided.

The calculations required to keep production focused on the items in accordance with the changing demands are described in the development of the critical ratio. The first portion of this ratio covers the effect of changing usage after the order is released.

A = Available stock / Recorder poitn quantity

This value should be less than 1.00 because the manufacturing order would not be written until the reorder point quantity is reached.

Method of Queuing: Any order from 0 to 1.00 should be given priority with those having the lowest ratio scheduled first. The orders with a 1.00:2.00 ratio should be worked on next, while those with ratios above 2.00 should be held up unless fill-in jobs are needed.

This system makes it inadvisable to release permanent wanted dates on either manufacturing orders or separate operations. Such dates would change so often it would be difficult to keep up with them. The priority is determined solely by the critical ratios as released on each successive queue list.

Work-load Adjustments. The conventional work loading will not be satisfactory with the ever-changing critical ratios.

We can assume that all jobs with a ratio under 1.00 should be completed within the lead time period. Though their priority may have changed slightly, it should not seriously affect the total load.

The jobs from 1.00 to 2.00 ratio will get some attention in the shop because if they didn't they would be picked up as critical before long. It might be necessary to reload jobs above a 1.50 ratio in some actual situations.

The jobs above a 2.00 ratio should always be reloaded in order to keep manufacturing realistically appraised of the task ahead.

In actual application, it may be desirable to print out the next one or two operations on the very critical jobs. This warning notice should be sent to the foremen in the areas concerned so that they can prepare to fit those jobs in on arrival.

The critical ratio method can also provide a calculation of the expected arrival time (EAT) based upon the current position of the order, its critical factor, and the amount of work ahead with lower critical, factors. This Eat notification may be important to the stock room, assembly personnel, and sales correspondents.

Further experience with critical ratio scheduling should lead to a reduction in safety stocks and possibly to a more continuous reassigning of work loads.

Where a summary of the critical ratio picture indicates that substantially more than 50 per cent are below 4.00, management should be alerted to major problems. This could be the net effect of a general increase in sales which requires a permanent or temporary change in corruptibilities, or it could come from supar performance in manufacturing.

Management should also watch specific areas in the plant where the critical ratios under 1.00 tend to predominate. These can be the trouble spots or bottleneck areas that can have a serious effect on the performance of the entire manufacturing function if they go uncorrected.

Monte carlo and simulation

Where it is not possible to make statistical studies from existing work flows, so-scale Monte Carlo techniques are available for determining lead time formulas. Here a very carefully selected sample of parts is used to represent simulated manufacturing conditions. End results can be studied by performing all successive operations "on paper", "processing part in the random sequence that would be expected in actual production, scheduling them through the various work variables. By repeating the simulation with different decision rules, the ones that bring about optimum results can be selected, even for a large variety of parts in a complex manufacturing situation. It is, of course, highly important that the data selected on a sampling basis are representative of thereal life situation, since the simulation obviously can be no better than the sample.

A number of programs are available from computer manufacturers to simulate production situations; it is also possible to have such an analysis made by a commercial computer service centre. The cost of liaving such simulation analyses made will normally be small in relation to the potential savings. However, because of the difficulty in the proper selection of the sample to be simulated, if it is possible to analyse the complete manufacturing plan by the statistical techniques previously discussed, the results from the latter could be more realistic than those obtained by simulation. Thus, in each situation the analyst has to choose between 100 per cent computer simulation or a manual Monte Carlo run using sampling techniques.

Where there is an equal choice of scheduling jobs that have the same end date, a high-low sequence based on the operational time involved provides the greatest chance of minimizing bottlenecks and maintaining a smooth flow. Any scheduling that tends to deviate to a wider degree from the statistical running average will tend to create more downstream waiting and pyramiding. One of the most serious problems in effective control is that of maintaining balanced flow and eliminating bottlenecks and idle time.

Linear programming

Linear programming provides opportunities for cost reduction where there are many cost alternatives to select from in either manufacturing or distribution. For a linear programming approach to be practical there must be a large number of elements or possibilities which present alternative choices, each choice with a different cost. When the choices are so numerous, usually in connection with scheduling a variety of products for different markets in different locations, that the least costly over-all plan is not immediately apparent, linear programming may be useful. Linear programming is a method for considering each possible alternative and selecting the choices that give the lowest total cost.

One use of linear programming is illustrated

by the following case. In this situation, many different grades of chemicals had to be manufactured each month and there were a number of different units upon which they could be manufactured, each with a different cost because of varying unit efficiencies. Each grade could be made on more than one unit; no one grade could be made on all units.

In order to determine whether savings in cost could be effected by use of linear programming, a three-month period was selected for comparison of costs by linear programming scheduling, as compared with actual scheduled costs.

The production demands of 17 grades on 16 units were scheduled individually for each of the three months concerned. To have developed a three-month schedule would have meant large savings, but since the company was operating on a month-to-month basis, three months' planning was not possible at the time.

Also, the basic data used accepted "demand" as those quantities actually scheduled by the production office without attempting any adjustment reflecting long-and short-range customer demand forecasts, inventory storage capabilities, and current inventory levels. It was assumed that the demand, as used, already reflected such considerations. This assumption did, therefore, simplify the over-all approach.

The linear program was run on a large computer with a program which has been used by leading airlines and petroleum companies. The use of a large computer assured adequate memory capacity as well as the availability of a tested program matrix.

Computer programming required the preparation of almost 1,000 IBM cards for later conversion to tape. Code sheets were prepared and from these, cards were punched. Five major groups of cards were included:

1. Direct costs
2. Demands for each grade for each of the three months.
3. Monthly capacity on each unit for each capable of production thereon.
4. Over-all monthly capacity for each unit
5. ID (identity) cards

The equations required for the program were already available on tape and called for no cards. Customer requirements for certain grades from specific units were inserted in the program by an adjustment of demand for indicated grades and of grade and over-all capacity for affected units.

Of particular importance in the accuracy of the computer assignment was the determination of practical over-all monthly unit capacities. As monthly capacities vary by grade on the same unit, it would be possible to overassign production if the over-all capacity were too large, and to undersign if the opposite were true. Therefore, the initial run was based on over-all unit capacities equal to the maximum grade capacity on the unit.

Equations used in the program reflected the major limitations imposed and the objectives. One limitation was that the amount of any one grade scheduled would be equal to the total demand during the month for that grade. Thus, for grade A on units 1 through 16:

$$A_1 + A_2 + \ldots + A_{16} = A$$

where A = total demand for grade A

A_1 = pounds of grade A scheduled on 1

A_2 = pounds of grade A scheduled on unit 2, etc.

A second limitation, obviously, was that the total pounds scheduled on any unit would not exceed the capacity of that unit for any month. Thus, for grades A through Q on unit 1:

$$A_1 + B_1 + \ldots + Q_1 < U_1$$

where U_1 = capacity of unit 1

A_1 = pounds of grade A scheduled on unit 1

B_1 = pounds of grade B scheduled on unit 1, etc.

The objective of the program was to arrive at the lowest possible direct cost production schedule. Therefore, the final equation into which all computations were worked—and the one indicating weather a new arrangement should be tried—became

Initial Run. As in any linear programming approach, the computer run, through a trial-and-error method, established a first feasible solution; that is, it arrived at a schedule which assigned the entire demand to available units without exceeding the capacities of these units. Then, proceeding from this point and following indicated product shift trends, the computer continued to set feasible total demand assignments representing succeedingly lower total direct costs until a lowest cost had been reached.

The advantages of a computer programming rather than a manual linear programming approach are in time and accuracy. The elapsed time for the computer to program the three months was slightly under five minutes. A conservative estimate of the time required to do the same number of computations manually would be several months. At the same number of computations manually would be several months At the same time, the probability of mathematical error in the manual method is high; in the computer run, it is considered to be non-existent.

Control of Computer Runs. Several runs were made on the computer. Following the first runs, unit capacities were reset to reduce possible overassignments. These adjustments were based on the apparent desired assignment by grade and were designed to permit a full month's production of the grade or grades assigned without overruns. In some instances this forced subsequent runs to shift overages to the next most desirable unit.

Comparative Analysis of Computer Production Assignments and the Production Office Schedule. The computer assignment of grades to units was compared with the original production office schedule with respect to (1) utilization of units and possible long-range scheduling benefits and (2) direct production costs. There were substantial savings in raw material and some in direct labour costs through long-range planning.

Analysis of the required unit day production showed that the three-month period the production office schedule with 1,288 unit days available had demands for 959 unit days or only 74.5 per cent of nominal capacity.

The computer, from a short-range aspect, could show little improvement in unit day assignment or labour saving because of the assignment of production and the interrelationships of certain unit operations, and because the demand reflected three short-term schedules rather than a long-range program. On the other hand, the computer linear program did indicate the benefits inherent in a long-range program. For example, the immediate shutting down of one unit and the curtailment of another early in the second month of the period would have been suggested by a long-range approach. In this case, the total unit days available would drop to 1,142, with demands using 1,004.5 or 88 per cent of total available capacity.

Cost Compressions: For each month, the total computer assignment cost is then compared with the comparable costs for the manner in which the production was scheduled by the production office.

Note that the raw materials savings for the three periods are $49,000, or approximately $200,000 per year, whereas the indicated total is only $40,000 for the three periods. However, from a practical standpoint, the increased labour costs, which theoretically had to be incurred in order to realize the raw materials savings, were not likely to materialize in this case. In no instance would more personnel have had to be hired to achieve the additional production at the newly assigned unit.

The UOM View of Linear Programming: Linear programming is another tool that can offer cost reduction in a number of cases. To obtain practical results, sound direct cost data and realistic input data and restrictions are required. The linear programming can become an integral part of the information and control system, projecting cost budgets for performance measurement as well as being an assignment technique. Too many companies have employed this and similar techniques as off-line programs rather than integrating them into the information and control plan.

Role of marketing in UOM

The marketing operation has two important functions within the general UOM framework. In addition to forecasting sales to obtain the optimum manufacturing plan, marketing management is responsible for using all available tools as effectively as possible to produce the most favourable combination of sales and profits. Whereas manufacturing is concerned essentially with the production of tangible items by definable methods with measurable ingredients, marketing is largely concerned with the many intangibles which are involved in buying decisions. The whole area of marketing is, therefore, less precise than manufacturing. Despite the fact that certain areas in marketing are more art than science, many new techniques have been developed to add to those already available for helping managers do a more effective marketing job. In this chapter we will be concerned only with the problem of optimization in marketing operations; that is, the second of the two marketing roles mentioned, since forecasting has already been discussed in the previous chapter.

To try to deal with all of the systematic procedures and scientific tools available for helping to do a more effective marketing job would require a book in itself. We will touch on several different areas, but we will concern ourselves mainly with techniques for developing and using the type of information required for both good forecasting and better sales planning and control.

The areas where various optimizing procedures can be used in marketing may be divided into the following general categories:

1. Determination of absolute and relative market potential
2. Maximization of direct and indirect sales effort

3. Advertising and promotional activity
4. Product strategy and pricing

The discussion in this chapter will be concerned with these four major headings.

Determination of market potential

In marketing, as in production and financial planning, utilization of the UOM concept requires the establishment of objectives and the measurement of results in terms of these objectives. The first step in the establishment of marketing objectives for a product line is to determine its market potential. By considering the potential market, taking into consideration past sales, competitive conditions, and other such factors, sales objectives can be established. These objectives should be set not just on an over-all basis, but by product, by sales territory, and by major customers.

Over-all product potential

The difficulty of determining the over-all potential for a product varies considerably from industry to industry. It also varies depending on the definition of potential. Thus, a company manufacturing room air conditioners might have concluded that the eventual potential for air conditioners was every room in every house in the United States. On this basis, the potential in any one year can be calculated from the number of homes in the United States at that time, the number of room per home, the number of air conditioners that have already been sold in previous years, and the replacement rate of air conditioners. Even on such an ideal formula as this, there can be some variation in estimates because of the uncertainty concerning the life of an air conditioner. Assuming that an air conditioner might last for fifteen to twenty years, it is still possible that a particular model could be made obsolete within a much shorter period of time. In fact, the room air conditioning units being produced today are so much smaller, require so much less current, are so much quieter and more efficient, that units produced ten years ago are virtually obsolete.

This type of potential may be of general interest in some industries, but is primarily useful to help calculate the degree of saturation of the market. Conclusions on the degree of saturation can, however, be quite deceptive. Many years ago people thought the market for radios would be exhausted when there was a radio in every home. This situation was changed with the introduction of small table radios, changed again by introduction of portables, and more recently by the introduction of transistorized portable radios. Product innovations can, therefore, have drastic effect on saturation rates.

Companies are usually most interested in estimating the total industry sales during the next year. In some industries, for example, the automotive industry, where figures are available on a weekly basis for production and where all cars have to be registered, it is relatively easy to determine total car production and sales in any year and also to discover the total number of cars on the road. There are other industries, however, where virtually no total industry data are available. Information on total production of particular products is available in considerable detail in the Census of Manufactures, which is published about every five years as well as in less detail in the annual Census publications. Many industries have trade associations which are in a position to publish comprehensive data on that particular industry on a regular basis. From such sources a company may be able to get a good idea of total sales or production of a particular product which they manufacture. In many cases, however, even when good industry data are available, the classification of the product is too broad to be useful for a particular company. For example, a company may produce kitchen tools such as spatulas, serving spoons, and strainers, but industry data may be released in the form of house-wares, including pots and pans, dish strainers, and a number of other items which the particular company does not produce.

If general industry data are not available, or are in such form that it is difficult to separate out a particular item which a company manufactures from a broader group, a company may get a feel for the total market situation from the regular annual statements of competitive companies. If the industry is one where there are not too many competitors, it is possible to put a ceiling on the total market by adding together all the competitor's sales figures. In most cases, to be sure, competitors will be making either a narrower or a broader product line, or will have products that will fall into several different product groups. Generally, statements of competitors will not be in sufficient detail for the reader to determine sales volume of individual products. The company can put a ceiling on the total volume but cannot be sure how much is represented by other products.

If industry and competitive data provide some broad-range estimates, it may be possible for a company to get a reasonably accurate size-up of the market by making a detailed survey in sleceted small areas. If reliable data can be obtained on total sales volume in these areas, the total volume can be projected on the basis of the relative importance of these areas to the country as a whole. Methods for determining the relationship of various areas of the country will be discussed in the next section.

Once a company has a good idea of the total industry sales volume, it should try to break the volume down by major competitors; then, by considering its own sales volume in comparison with the relative strength of competition in various areas, it becomes possible to begin to establish some sales objectives. While a first attempt at establishment of a sales objective can be made on an over-all basis, realistic objectives can only be established through more detailed analysis, area-by-area, territory-by-territory, and customer-by-customer.

Relative market potential

Consumer Products: The first step in the determination of relative market potential, that is, the importance of one area versus another, is the selection of some general index. There are a number of published indexes of potential. For consumer products the most widely used is probably Sales Management's Survey of Buying Power. Sales Management annually publishes figures by states, by major countries, by metropolitan areas, and by principal cities showing estimates of population, retail sales, number of families, buying power per family, and other data. The figures check quite closely with the government census figures in the census years. Sales Management has constructed an index of potential based on the population, retail sales, and family income or buying power. Each of these elements is weighted and combined with the others to give an index which is then expressed in terms of percentage of total United States. For many consumer products, this Sales Management index will provide an excellent rough yardstick of potential for each county and city.

For other products it may be necessary either to adjust this index or to construct an entirely new one. For example, a company may manufacture a product that is affected considerably by the climate. Thus, heavy clothing would not be expected to sell as well in the South as in the North; or a company might manufacture a product that depends upon a certain raw material, such as a gas furnace. Sales of gas furnaces are likely to be influenced significantly not only by the climate, but also by the relative cost of gas, oil, coal, and electricity in any particular area. By analysis of its product, a company can determine if factors such as these are likey to influence sales by areas and proceed to construct its own relative index of potential, taking into account factors in addition to population, buying power, and retail sales, which influence product sale.

Industrial Products. The problem of determining the relative potential for an industrial product is quite different from that for a consumer product. The industrial product is sold to other manufacturers; therefore, it is the location of these manufacturers rather than the public, generally, that is of importance.

The basic source of information about location of manufacturing operations in the U.S. is the Census of Manufactures. The Census of Manufactures divides all manufacturing industry into 21 major categories-so-called two-digit industry categories suh as: "34, fabricated metal products" or "35, machinery except electrical", then further subdivides each of these into a three-digit, four-digit, and down to seven-digit categories, each being a breakdown of the preceding larger category. Some total information is available about total production of certain seven-digit industries, but information on a regional basis is broken down only to four-digit industries. There are 426 four-digit categories of manufacturing industries. For each of these industries, information is available about number of manufacturing plants, number of employees, number of productive employees, cost of materials, value added by manufacture, and value of shipments. In many cases, however, this detailed information is not available on a county basis. A particular county may have only one or two industries in the same four-digit category and if the Census were to publish all figures, each company could discover the other's pertinent data by simply subtracting its own figures from the total published by the Census. The Census, therefore, will publish figures only if there are three or more companies of a particular four-digit category in a country. Although figures on value of shipments, cost of materials, etc., are not shown in cases where there are less than three companies, the *Census* does indicate the number of companies and usually the number of employees in each county.

In addition to the Census of Manufactures, a number of states publish breakdowns for manufacturing industries by counties and cities within the state. There is considerable variation from state to state in the kind of information that is published and in the timelines and accuracy of the data. Some publications use the same Standard Industrial Classification (SIC) used by the Census. Others have their own industry breakdown. In addition, the local chambers of commerce of many cities have a detailed breakdown of all manufacturing companies such as Dun & Bradstreet, Fortune magazine and Sales Management magazine, which give information about manufacturing establishments on a city and country basis.

Sales Management magazine has tried to tap all available sources of information in all important counties and cities in the United States to update the Census of Manufactures information and made a breakdown by counties including four-digit categories which the census deos not include for disclosure reasons. Such information is on NIVAC tapes and can be purchased in various forms from Sales Management magazine.

To use any of these data for determination of relative market potential, it is necessary for a company, by analyzing its own sales, to find out to which four-digit industries it sells. The first step in this analysis is to classify customers in order of size. As previously noted, it will be discovered that in most companies, 20 to 25 per cent of the customers account for 75 to 80 per cent of total sales volume. Each customer in this major customer group should be classified into four-digit SIC categories. It may then be desirable to select a random sample of the smaller customers and classify them in a similar fashion. Only the four-digit categories containing customers will then be used in constructing the potential index.

Some industries will be more important to a company than others—not so much because the industry is larger, but because it has a greater need for the company's products. Thus, a manufacturer of leather might sell only a small amount to a big electronics company but a large amount to a small manufacturer of shoes. In order to make statistics of manufacturing companies meaningful, a company must have some method of weighting the various industries in terms of their importance as prospective customers.

One such method is to relate the company's sales to an industry to the number of employees in the industry. Through checking with the salesmen who call on the customers and through the use of various sources such as state industry data books, Dun & Bradstreet, Sales Management, and others, the number of employees in each of the plants of these customers can be determined. Then company sales can be expressed in terms of sales per employee in each four-digit category. By finding the number of employees in all the selected four-digit categories in each county, and retating this number of the total of all employees in the United States in these selected four-digit categories, a first rough approximation will be obtained for the relative importance of each county. By then weighting the figures in each four-digit category in each county in terms of its relative importance in sales per employee and relating the weighted figure in each county to the weighted United States total, a better index of potential will be available.

This index will provide a rough guide, but will need further refinement. There are two principal weakneses in the index in this form. First, the sales of the particular company to various industries may be unrepresentative of the way competition sells; for example, there may be some very important industries to whom competition sells which are relatively unimportant for this particular company. The first refinement in the index, therefore, will require determining total sales of company and competitive product to all major customers and expressing total volume of such sales to each customer in terms of number of employees.

The second weakness lies in the fact that the four-digit industry category is in itself a catchall. Virtually all a company's sales may go to a seven-digit industry within the four-digit category. The geographical location of the seven-digit group may be quite different from that of the over-all four-digit category. A company should plan, therefore, to refine continually the index which it establishes initially.

For most companies the first rough index constructed along the lines suggested will prove useful. For many companies it will be most advantageous to put the data for the four-digit category representing potential customers on punched cards, showing the country, number of plants, number of employees, and weighted number of employees. By sorting the cards by sales territory, it will then be possible to determine the relative importance of each sales territory and each county within each sales territory. All figures should be expressed in terms of percentage of the whole United States; sales in each county and territory in terms of percentage of total sales can then be compared wth this index.

While the index can be refined and improved along the lines suggested, unquestionably the first time sales are compared with the index, some significant variation will immediately become apparent. The comparison will probably suggest that certain territories, which on the basis of total dollar sales appear to be very good, do not show up so well when compared with the sales that might be expected on the basis of the index of potential. Salesmen's performance in certain territories undoubtedly will be revealed as much better than realized.

An index of this sort can be an exceedingly useful tool. It must, however, be used carefully, for some of the reasons suggested, a rough index may be quite inaccurate. It should be looked on initially, therefore, as a guide rather than as a measure. If the comparison of sales with potential suggests that a particular territory is weak and another is strong, an analysis in depth should be made of these two territories to discover whether the analysis will support this first conclusion.

Some rough checks can often be made quite quickely. For example, in one company where we had worked with management to set up such an index of potential, the comparison of actual with potential suggested that in one major area of the country the company was doing a relatively good job and in another area a relatively poor job. The sales manager, through discussion with the salesmen in the two regions, determined exactly how many competitive salesmen were working in each area. In the area where his company appeared to be doing a comparatively good job, he discovered the number of his salesmen in the region, compared with all salesmen in the region, was substantially higher than in the other area where the company was doing a poor job relative to potential. The sales manager not only got another bit of information that tended to substantiate the index of potential, but also had an indication that sales could be increased in the poorer territory by increasing the number of salesmen.

Another use of the index is to help translate the potential within a particular county into specific firms. Thus, if in salesman A's territory the index shows that there are 50 companies in the county in eight different four-digit industry categories, the salesman should start identifying these companies. Some of these will be customers and will be identified immediately; others will be on the salesman's prospect list; still others will be unknown to the salesman. Through the state books or the individual listings provided by cities, the salesman can determine which companies are involved and visit them. By tracking down all the large indicated potential customers, the salesman will undoubtedly learn about many new potential accounts and will, at the same time, improve the effectiveness of the index by eliminating any companies that do not represent possible future business.

Establishment of sales objectives

As indicated in the previous section, a considerable amount of sales analysis is involved in the creation of the relative index of potential. The primary objective of sales analysis is the development of the greatest possible sales volume at the smallest cost and greatest profit through greater knowledge and understanding of prospects and customers. With a relative index of potential, the sales manager and his salesman have a starting point with which to begin a more detailed analysis of each territory. An analysis of territories by customers is required in order to establish reasonable annual sales objectives and to then exercise effective control over performance. The establishment of sales objectives is one of the prime elements in a UOM operation.

Development of territorial objectives

The development of over-all annual objectives should take into account:

1. Number and size of current and potential customers
2. Past use of the company's products by current and potential customers
3. General business trends which are likely to have favourable and unfavourable impact on probable sales by any or all of the users.
4. Specific customer plans or programs which will affect the use of the company's product during the year.

Theoretically, it would be desirable to make an analysis of every potential customer in a territory, but carrying the analysis to such an extreme is seldom practical. A progressive analysis of the potential users in a territory, starting with the largest ones, is recommended. Although this may appear to be a big job for the salesman and his superiors, the benefits through more effective planning in territory coverage will more than offset the effort required.

Since the salesman should know customers and prospects in his territory better than anyone else, the initial analysis should be prepared by the salesman, then checked in detail by his immediate superviser. Finally, the sales manager should review each territory. Both the sales supervisor and the sales manager will be able to supplement and improve upon the information provided by the salesman.

Analysis of Customers and Prospects. The following steps are suggested to establish sales goals by products for the coming year:

Step 1: List all current accounts on a form.

Step 2: Enter actual dollar purchases for each account for the last two years.

Step 3: Based on purchases to date in the current year, enter the probable total purchases from the company during the entire year.

Step 4: Based on the salesman's acquaintance with each account and his knowledge of his approximate share of their total purchases of similar products, estimate the probable total use of his own and competitive products for each of the three years.

Step 5: Taking into consideration past and present activities, general business conditions in the particular area and industry, and any known specific customer plans for expansion or constraction, estimate each account's probable total use of the company's and competitive products for the coming year.

Step 6: Based on this probable total annual use and past sales, as well as plans for the coming year, estimate probable sales to each account.

Step 7: Rate each account as to its probable purchase of the company's product. The largest customer should have an A rating, the next a B, and so on down to F. Similarly, each account should be rated in terms of its probable total use of products similar to those manufactured by the company. Thus, the largest purchasers should be in Group 1, the next in Group 2, and so on down. There, thus, are two key ratings- one in terms of actual purchases from the company, and one in terms of total use of products similar to that manufactured by the company. It is conceivable that a customer might be rated as Group 1 in terms of its total use of products under consideration, but rated F because it purchases very little from the company.

In addition to developing information about present customers, the same procedure should be carried out in connection with manufacturers who are potential customers, but who have not actually purchases, or are not purchasing at the present time, from the company. Information should be written on the same type form as follows:

Step 1: List all potential accounts not currently customers.

Step 2: Checking the potential customers against sales tabulations, enter any sales made to such customers during the last two years.

Step 3: Based on the present sales program, indicate any probable sales which might be made to any potential customer during the balance of the current year.

Step 4: Based on knowledge of each account and any additional information that may be obtained through industry contacts, estimate the total use of company and competitive products for each of the three years.

Step 5: Taking into consideration past and present activities, general industrial conditions in the particular area, and any known specific customer plans, estimate each potential customer's probable total use of products under consideration for the coming year.

Step 6: Based on this probable total annual use

and the salesman's plan for the coming year, make an estimate of the sales objective for each account.

Step 7: Rate each account as to its probable purchases of the company's product.

Step 8: Rate each account as to its probable total use of products similar to those manufactured by the company.

This account-by-account analysis, including prospects to whom the company is not selling as well as those to whom it is, is very important. It can highlight for the salesman and the sales manager, in a manner impossible in any other way, the importance of broadening the sales coverage. It can also open the eyes of the salesman about potential business that is being missed. Unless salesman activitely attempted to learn about accounts to whom they are not selling, the temptation is very great merely to continue to call on the same old customers.

In many cases, just locating potential customers is a task in itself. The relative index of potential is very useful in this connection because it contains the number of plants in particular four-digit industry categories that presumably represent potential business. The salesman can track down the various accounts to determine whether they do, in fact, represent potential for the company's product.

One client was initially reluctant to accept the idea that anything could be learned from indexes of potential and from such extensive analysis as outlined. The company had been in business for many years and was obtaining a significant share of the total market for its product. The salesmen, the regional sales managers, and the general sales manager all felt that they knew their customers and their prospects and that little could be gained from a full-scale analysis. Nonetheless, the procedure indicated in the above paragraph was followed; each salesman listed the company sales and total indicated use of the company's product for each important customers or prospective customer. Because no one in the company was convinced that this procedure offered any real assistance, it took many months before all the data could be assembled. When they were finally ready, the total business represented by the salesman's estimate of each customer's total purchases of products similar to those manufactured by the company was added. The total, which represented all of the potential business that the entire sales force knew anything about, came to less than half of the known total market for the company's product. The figures for the total market were quite reliable and could be checked out in several different ways.

When the totals were shown to the sales manager and compared with total industry figures, his reaction was amazement. He and all the salesmen had firmly believed that they knew where over 80 per cent of the market was located; yet the figures showed that the company actually knew about only half of the total potential market. For the first time, the company really began to see the possibilities of market analysis. It was obvious that there were a number of large accounts about which salesmen knew nothing or else salesmen were getting a much smaller share of present customers' business than they believed. Oven the next few months, both possibilities were pursued. As a result, many new large prospective customers were revealed and, in addition, the company found that it was obtaining a smaller share of the business of many large accounts than the salesmen had believed.

For each salesman, specific targest were established in terms of a few of the principal accounts. In each territory, five or six large prospective accounts were listed with an objective of getting a specific amount of business from each. These accounts were called "target accounts" and procedure was established throughout the company for special handling of all correspondence relating to "target accounts".

As a result of the effort over the next year, the company substantially improved its competitive position in the industry. At the time when competitors were experiencing declining sales and profits, this company expanded its sales and profits.

Preparation of Customers Cards. Using the same form under the frequency of call columns, each salesman should indicate, for each account and each prospect on the list, the total number of calls to be made during the year and the average length of a call. In making these estimates, he should consider the account rating, geographical location or accessibility of the account, and other pertinent information about the account such as the people who have to be called on, their manner of purchasing, etc. Many buyers have particular preferences as to how frequency they like to see salesmen and how much time they will spend with them. Thus, one account might require eight 1/2 hour calls during the year; whereas another would require two 4-hour calls. The salesman should indicate the coverage that, in his opinion, will best assure a profitable relationship with the account.

It may be desirable to reproduce such cards in punched-card form for subsequent sorting and tabulation at the head office. It is important, however, for each salesman to have his own set of cards. The salesman should be concerned not only with total dollar sales but also with the breakdown of sales to each account by product. For each account, he should indicate the various products that are purchased from the company. Presumably, in most companies this information will be made available to the salesmen on a regular basis from the central office. In some companies, however, the salesmen keep track of sales by product either roughly or in total on the basis of copies of invoices which they receive. Fundamentally, the same procedure should be followed with each of the product lines purchased by the customer as indicated previously for total dollar sales. In other words, the salesman should have a record of the purchases from his company of particular products as well as the total use of such prducts by a company or prospect.

Summarizing the Data. As a preliminary step, all accounts should be grouped as key accounts, secondary accounts, and supporting accounts. This grouping should be made for both active accounts and potential accounts. The key accounts are those groups purchasing quantities that would put them in the A and B categories by size, or in the 1, 2, and 3 groups in terms of potential. Secondary accounts would include customers in Group C or potential customers in Group 4. Supporting accounts would be the other accounts and prospects not in the preceding two groups.

The best way to get accounts lined up in these ways is by actual sorting of the individual account cards. First, the active account cards should be sorted into six Groups: A, B, C,D, E and F. The A and B Groups should be set aside as key accounts and, similarly, the prospective account cards sorted into 1, 2, 3, 4, 5, and 6 Groups. Within the active account card group, some sorting will be done in addition to the sort by sales in terms of the potential rating. Thus, an account which fell into Group D on the basis of purchase, but was in group 1 or 2 in terms of its potential, would be in the key account class.

The analysis of accounts and prospects described should be performed by each salesman working with his immediate superior. Unquestionably, there will be changes in the figures for estimated potential of any account and the salesman's estimated share of that potential. After the salesman's immediate superior has gone over these figures and made some adjustments, regional sales management and, finally, general sales management may make further changes. In some cases the home office may know more about the total purchases of a large customer than the salesman, or may be in a better position to estimate the total potential represented by a prospect who has not been purchasing from the company. After the information has been examined and refined, the figures from each territory can be combined to get an over-all sales forecast in total and by product. This detailed account-by-account forecast can then be compared with other forecasts based on statistical forecasting procedures and general industry analysis. While the statistical product forecast will probably prove a better working tool for production planning, it will be the detailed account-by-account analysis that will prove most useful in directing the sales effort during the year to reach the goals.

Planning account coverage

Once having calculated rough sales objectives for each account, it is necessary to prepare a plan for attaining these objectives. This means developing a general plan for the coming year in each territory which will afford effective account coverage and economical use of time. This will require consideration of a number of influencing factors and a certain amount of juggling of sales call schedules before a workable coverage plan is developed. Among the factors that must be borne in mind are the number of calls to make on each account and the buying habits of various accounts, for example, whether the account purchases on a quarterly, monthly, or yearly basis.

Starting with the account cards and using the territory sales coverage schedule form the sales call requirements for each territory should be spread out for the coming year by area, town, active and prospective account group, frequency and length of call. This spreading out of the call requirements will (1) indicate the feasibility of covering all accounts with a desired frequency, (2) pinpoint the relationship between contact of current active accounts and missionary workwith prospective customers, and (3) stress those frequency groups where specific consideration on when should this call be made- June, November, January, etc. The following detail steps should then be applied:

Step 1: Sort all account cards, keeping active and prospect cards separate by state and city or town.

Step 2: Group these cards by area.

Step 3: Sort account cards for each town, again keeping active and prospective customers separate by desired calls per year.

Step 4: Record this information on the territory sales coverage schedule. For each town, the number of active and prospective accounts which fall under each call per year heading should be indicated. For each group of cards, the approximate total time in days to cover all accounts should be indicated.

Then for each month calculate the approximate time in days to be allowed for additional travel time, special activities such as trade conventions, district or company sales meetings, holiday and vacations, and time which from experience should be allowed to handle unusual emergencies. When all these figures plus the call figures are totalled, they can be compared with the available working days in the month concerned. The schedule can then be reexamined and readjusted to bring coverage into line with available time.

Assuming that territories have been laid out correctly in the first place, as a result of this analysis a working plan is available for meeting the sales objectives established.

Control

Since accurate forecasting is such an essential element is Unified Operations Management, it is important that company management understand its own requirements and develop the methods and techniques that will permit good forecasting. Predicting the movements of the United States and world economy has become a major activity of many business economists and economic consultants. The Federal government itself is deeply involved in forecasting activities of all types. Yet, despite the prevalence of forecasting in our economy today, many businessmen shy away from it in their own business; or, if they do project business activity for their concern, they are not confident enough of their forecasts to use them effectively.

For Unified Operations Management purposes the initial responsibility for forecasting belongs to the marketing organization, which is closest to the customers and in the best position to be aware of future trends likely to influence business. While marketing management in many companies is willing to accept its responsibilities for general forecasting of probable total dollar sales, it has been reluctant to attempt detailed, specific product-by-product, item-by-item forecasts. Yet, for manufacturing purposes only such a detailed forecast is of value. Since a manufacturing organization is responsible for making specific units of particular products, an over-all dollar forecast is of little practical use.

Although marketing people may not believe it is possible to predict in such specific terms, in practically all companies such an activity is necessary although it may not go under the name of forecasting. The manufacturing organization must plan ahead before it schedules production of various items. Frequently, schedules are based on the routine decisions of clerks who will indicate the requirements determined by some relationship between stock on hand, lead time, and average requirements in the past. A company with such a system is forecasting, though no one in the organization may designate the planning by this name.

Varying forecast requirements

In our opinion, one of the principal problems many companies experience with forecasts results from a failure to recognize that different departments or functions in a company have different requirements for a forecast. Thus, as discussed above, the manufacturing organization requires a specific forecast of requirements for individual products and units. Manufacturing has to plan the production and schedule the volume of the items to be produced at different times on various machines. Particularly in the use of Unified Operation Management techniques, manufacturing must be able to forecast requirements for some period in advance—this period varying from a month to a year—in such a way that costs will be minimized and profits maximized. Manufacturing's requirement, therefore, is for a forecast that is specific as to individual units for a specified period in the future.

Even for a manufacturing operation, however, the needs will vary considerably from one company to another. The basic determinant is the type of manufacturing operation and the economic advantages of being able to forecast accurately for each additional period in the future. In some companies, it may be possible to effect practically of the savings that can be realized through forecasting if a month's requirement can be projected into the future. In another company, it may not be possible to effect any particular savings unless it is possible to predict as far ahead as six months.

Thus, in one large processing company, it appeared possible to make significant savings in a certain process through the use of linear programming. One of the major areas of savings would arise from shutting down particular units in the process and operating other units at capacity. If units were to be shut down, however, they had to be down for as long as six months at a time in order to effect savings through reduction in operating labour. A forecast of the total volume of products that would be produced on these units was therefore required for at least this period of time.

On the other hand, a number of grades of material could be made on these same units with relatively low change-over costs from one grade to another. Most of the savings that could be realized through effective use of particular units for particular grades could be obtained by forecasting a month in advance. Thus, for this company, it was necessary to forecast a general level of operations for six months at a time but only to forecast individual grade requirements a month ahead.

The first step in forecasting requirements for manufacturing, therefore, is to determine for what period a forecast is necessary. In most companies it will be discovered that while, theoretically, substantial savings could be realized if it were possible to forecast accurately for a year or two in advance, the great portion of such savings can be obtained if forecasts are accurate for much shorter periods.

Other functions of a business require forecasts for different purposes. The marketing organization, for example, needs a forecast in order to determine marketing strategy. By forecasting the sales of particular products and determining the marginal income expected from such sales, management may decide to drop the particular products, add a new product, change the promotional and selling emphasis from one product to another, or lower prices. Forecasts of sales and costs are also essential for determining the general level of advertising and promotional expenditures and selling costs. For most purposes, however, the degree of accuracy required for a saless forecast is less precise than for a materials requirements manufacturing forecast.

Another important purpose of a forecast for the marketing organization is to establish sales budgets and sales objectives. These sales objectives may be used to establish quotas for individual territories for various products and for products to be sold by a particular salesman. Such quotas may also be tied into an incentive plan for salesmen's compensation.

The financial department will require forecasts in order to establish current operating budgets for the various parts of the business, and as a guide toward estimating requirements for cash and credit. Longer-term forecasts are needed in order to plan for new plants and equipment. Since it may take a year or two after deciding that a new plant is required before production can actually begin, it is essential that forecasts be projected sufficiently far in the future to provide this type of guidance.

The degree and the type of accuracy required for the different parts of the business in forecasting vary considerably. Let us consider for a moment the effect on the marketing and manufacturing organizations of a significant error in a forecast. Let us assume that there was a 50 per cent error in the forecast of one product and a 25 per cent error in another. Because of the different prices of these products, however, the sales lost from the overestimate of requirements by 50 per cent of product A were exactly compensated for by the underestimate of the requirements for product B. Thus, the forecast was accurate for total dollars sales. The marketing organization of a company might be perfectly happy with the total dollar forecast and could conceivably show the same gross margin and the same expenditures.

A manufacturing organization would be most unhappy about such failures in forecasting, however, since it would have produced 50 per cent too much of one product and 25 per cent too little of another. It would have been extremely important, therefore, for manufacturing to know as soon as there was any evidence that the initial forecast for product A was too optimistic so that corrective action could be taken immediately. Similarly, manufacturing would want to know immediately when evidence was available that sales were going much better for product B in order to revise its production upward.

The marketing organization should expect to utilise sales information at the earliest date to get the sales force to put forth special effort to bring the sales back to the forecast. It probably would not be desirable to change the sales forecast, as far as marketing was concerned, but marketing might be able to bring sales more closely in line with the forecast.

Although the needs of the different parts of the organization vary, it is important to avoid having each part of the company produceits own independent forecast. In the beginning, a forecast should be developed that is acceptable to the various parts of the organization. It may be changed for different departments as actual data come in, but the requirements plan for production, the financial forecast, and the sales budget should all be tied into the original forecast. If changes in one are made during the course of the year, but not in another, the reason for a change should be clear-cut, based on regular procedures and easily reconcilable with the figures being used by the other departments.

In considering a forecast in a company,

therefore, it is important to determine what the forecast needs are for different departments in the organization, how long and how accurate a forecast is required, and what change in budgets will be made as a result of changes in anticipated volume.

The external forecast

The importance of external forecasting—that is, forecasting company sales by looking at figures of other kinds, such as those for the industry of which the company is a part, the anticipated activity of those industries making up the major customers of the company, anticipated Gross National Product or the volume of one of its major sectors—will vary from company to company. In the major rubber companies, the forecast of Gross National Product and the number of new automobiles likely to be produced for the next year will be exceedingly important because automobile tires represent a major end use for rubber. At the other extreme, a manufacturer of a new gadget or novelty will not be particularly interested in such data as Gross National Product or even department store sales. He will be concerned solely with the possibility of his gadget's attracting popular fancy.

Most companies will be somewhere in between these extremes. Sales will be significantly influenced by various outside factors, such as the general state of the economy and specific demands of customers for industrial products, but there will be a considerable variable element that will be related to the effectiveness of the selling effort and the attractiveness of the product relative to competition. It is important that a company analyze its products and decide which factors are most important in influencing their sales volume—those factors over which they have control, such as product design, advertising, and promotion and sales efforts, or those factors over which they have relatively little control, such as demands of coustomers and the general state of the economy. Quite conceivably, within any particular company the balance may be in one direction for some products and in the opposite direction for others.

Ideally, a company would like to find some type of lead indicator; in other words, a series regularly available that goes up and down in the same fashion as company sales but a month or two in advance. If such an indicator can be located, the company is in an optimum position particularly for short-range forecasting. Unfortunately, companies rarely find a lead indicator for which data are regularly available soon enough to be useful.

While use of Gross National Product or one of the major components may well be helpful in developing an individual company forecast, it seldom seems advisable to attempt to forecast GNP independently, but rather to use one of the forecasts made by specialists in this type of prediction. Various organizations devote their full time to prediction of Gross National Product and component parts. Some companies of this type have established sophisticated models with great quantities of data on various portions of the economy which are fed into a computer to produce a forecast. Other forecasters follow a somewhat simpler procedure but still manage to produce good forecasts. If a company is going to pay for the services of one of these forecasting organizations, we suggest that its past record of forecasting be compared with what actually happened in the economy to determine how effective it has been, regardless of the methods used. If it does not seem economical to pay for a regular forecasting service, there are any number of other individuals and organizations who make a regular practice of preparing for general publication their forecasts of Gross National Product and even of some of the major components.

Forecasts of Gross National Product and its components may be of immediate use to a company in forecasting its own sales, but probably such forecasts will be used merely to provide a general framework within which more specific forecasts will be made. For some industries general industry data are very good, either as a result of industry association activity or because the product line fits very closely to one of the general census categories. In such cases there may be specific forecasts made by industry groups which will be immediately useful to a company. In other situations a company's product line is so diversified that individual forecasts are needed for several different industries.

While there are many variations that might

be encountered, consider the situation of a company which manufactures an industrial rather than a consumer product for which industry data are occasionally but not regularly available, and for which no industry forecast is available from outside. How would such a company go about preparing a forecast?

Preparing an annual forecast

The first step is to analyze the company's sales by customers. This task is not as formidable as it sounds, if customers are first ranked by dollar volume purchased. In almost every company it will be found that 20 to 25 per cent of the customers account for 75 to 80 per cent, or more, of total sales volume. Initially, therefore, these large customers are classified into various industry categories as established by the Bureau of the Census in its Standard Industrial Classification (SIC) of industries. This will probably involve, for some companies, consultation with the salesman who sells to the customer to learn just what the customer's business actually is and, if possible, what use it makes of the product. Such an analysis in many companies will probably indicate that comparatively few industries represent the most important use of the company's product.

Next, these major industries are examined to get all the data possible about their sales activities during the last five to ten years and any data that is available indicating what is likely to happen to their business in the next few years. In some of these industries, sales volume is probably rising faster than Gross National Product or the particular component of which they are a part as, for example, durable goods or nondurable goods. Other industries sales are rising less rapidly, and still others are going at about the same rate as the important component to which they relate in Gross National Product. Based on the trends of performance of these companies relative to major components of Gross National Product for which forecasts are available, a forecast is made for each of these major industries for the next twelve months. Then sales in previous years are analyzed to find out whether an industry's purchases of the company's products are going up or down relative to the industry's activity.

Later it may prove desirable to make a more extensive analysis in collaboration with individual salesmen to determine more about customers' purchases of similar competitive products. It may well be that industries which were not included in the major customer group are important; or sales may be relatively small to customers in an industry which is purchasing large volumes from competitors. Eventually, industries should be ranked by their purchases not only by the specific product but by the general type of product. For initial forecasting purposes, however, analysis of the company's sales to these various industries will be of major importance. Once a forecast has been prepared of the major industries to whom the company sells and they are rated in terms of importance as customers, a forecast of the company's sales for the next twelve months can be made.

For some companies it is essential that attention be given not only to the United States market but to the world market situation. For example, company A is a major factor in the United States domestic market and normally exports 25 to 30 per cent of domestic production. At the same time, in plants in a variety of foreign countries, the company produces and sells virtually as much as it sells in the United States domestic market. This company must be concerned with forecasting industry trends on a worldwide basis. It follows a procedure similar to the one described above for forecasting requirements in the domestic market. It then develops a forecast of industry requirements in each of the foreign countries in which it has a plant. Since in most foreign countries its own and competitive plants are operating at capacity, the economist determines probable United States exports for the coming year by subtracting production capacity available in foreign countries from the anticipated demand in those countries. The difference between these figures is the probable level of United States exports.

Other companies will approach the world situation in different ways. Most will find that data on production in foreign countries are less readily available than in the United States. On the other hand, for some situations specific information relating to exports and imports may be accurate and timely.

By the use of external data a company tries to

establish some basis for predicting its own sales for the coming year. All forecasting is primarily a process of looking at past performance, seeing what the trends are, and trying to predict what will happen in the future based on the best judgment and estimates of future demands. By getting information about the future of the economy which has proved generally reliable and by getting more specific information about the indicated future activity of important industries to which the company sells, it attempts to build up explanations of the probable course of its sales during the next period.

In some situations management may reach the conclusion that it is better to make a judgement about future sales of the company itself than to try to make similar judgments about a number of less familiar industries. In many cases, however, the analysis of sales to a particular industry and the analysis of that industry's own sales will reveal important trends which may continue, regardless of short-range fluctuations relating to the general economic picture. In such cases a company is likely to have a much better understanding of the probable future of its own sales than if it did not make this type of analysis.

Forecasting by Quarters and Months. While the forecast for the next twelve months will be valuable to all parts of the organization. most functional groups will require some indication of how the annual volume is likely to be spread out in terms of months and quarters. Two elements are important in this connection. One is the general underlying secular and cyclical trends as revealed by analysis of the industry as a whole and important customer groups. The other is any seasonal pattern that may be peculiar to the company. Presumably the trends will have been discovered in making the general forecast. In other words, most forecasts for the economy as a whole indicate whether the rise is likely to be strong in the first quarter or first half, whether it is likely to continue during the third and fourth quarters, or whether things are likely to taper off. If there are no clear-cut indications along these lines, a company can probably concluded that as far as the cyclical influence is concerned the annual forecast can be divided into four parts.

It is vitally important to discover, however, the seasonal pattern of a company. This pattern can be determined by plotting sales for a number of years in the past. Sales for about the last five years should be shown on a monthly basis on the same graph, one superimposed on the othe. Where newer products are involved, two years can be used and deviations can be adjusted yearly. If there is any distinct seasonal pattern, it will show up immediately from this graphical presentation.

An average can then be taken for all the Januarys, all the Februarys, all the Marches, etc., for a number of years to determine how much of the annual volume is represented by each month of the year. The twelve; this "average month" can be considered 100, and the sales for each month expressed in terms of this average as greater or less than 100. Once a monthly index has been constructed in this way, the annual forecast can be broken down into months and quarters by applying the index for each month to the annual forecast.

In the construction of this index a certain amount of judgment must be used, if there has been a drastic change in a company's product line during the period. Clearly, the early years of the period must be disregarded and only the later years, where the products are similar to those now in existence, should be used in construction of the seasonal index.

It is not unlikely that different products in the lines will have different seasonal indexes. An index must then be constructed for each product line rather than using an averaging process.

Limitations of external forcast

The forecast resulting from the analysis of external data may be adequate for sales planning and establishment of sales objectives. It may also be satisfactory for financial planning. It is not likely, however, to meet the requirements of manufacturing because it is seldom specific enough in terms of individual items in a product line for production planning. In all probability the result of the type of forecast we have described would be to establish a projection of dollars sales for a broad product line. For a machine tool company it may produce an estimate of the dollar volume of a company's line of lathes, but production must know how many lathes of each particular size will be required. Thus, the forecast is not specific enough for production planning.

Another important weakness in the forecast as produced so far is that there is no procedure for indicating when the forecast has gone wrong and for making adjustments in it. It is not possible to forecast with 100 per cent accuracy. There will be some random variations from month to month, even in a forecast that turns out to be 95 per cent accurate over a year. It is important that some control limits be established above and below the forecast by months that will indicate when a forecast is out of control and when an adjustment is necessary.

By combining material obtained from the forecast made on the basis of external data with various statistical analysis of past data, it is possible for most companies to develop specific product-by-product forecasts and to establish control limits for these forecasts.

Short-run statistical forecasting

Probably the most common statistical tool used for projecting past data into the future is some form of moving average. A moving average is one that literally moves or changes as data for each new period are developed. Thus, a six months' moving average would be compiled as follows: in January, figures for the months July through December would be averaged. When January's data became available, July would be dropped from the series and the new six months' moving average would be for the months August through January.

Similarly, when February's figures were obtained, August's figures would be dropped.

The effect of such a moving average is to smooth out the peaks and valleys. A moving average always tends to lag somewhat behind the most current data since the current data have a weight in a six months' moving average of only one-sixth. The longer the series, for example, a twelve months' or twenty-four months' moving average, the less effect the most recent data have on the total. The shorter the series—a six months' or a three months' moving average—the more closely the average will follow the latest figures.

To use a simple moving average for forecasting, one can assume that the latest moving average is the best indication of what will happen in the next period. Thus, if the figures are available for January, February and March, the moving average of January's 100, February 120, and March's 110 would be 110; therefore, 110 is the best estimate for April. Assuming April's figure is actually 106, the new moving average would be 112 and the forecast for May would be 112.

It should be noted that the use of the moving average for forecasting does not take into account any factors that may be known or presumed about the future. It merely takes as average for the past which may be indicative of a trend and assumes that it is going to continue in the future. The prime advantage of this type of statistical tool is that it presents a new forecast each period based upon the latest information available.

Exponential smoothing

A moving average is sometimes awkward to work with because of the necessity of keeping figures available for each month in the past forming a part of the average. The equivalent of a moving average can be obtained by a device called exponential smoothing. With exponential smoothing it is only necessary to use two figures, the past average and the current data. Thus, for the equivalent of the three months' moving average described above, the average for the months January, February, and March of 110 is divided by two, and half of the figure for April added. The average obtained this way would be 108, close to the three month's moving average of 112 calculated.

Using an exponential smoothing formula rather than keeping track of the months for a moving average calculation is particularly desirable where a computer is used to calculate the averages. The computer need keep only the last average in storage rather than a string of months from the past. This storage factor becomes particularly important if a computer is keeping track of many thousands of items.

Selection of average

The question of the kind of moving average to use for a particular company can be answered only by analysing past data. In doing so, the first question to keep in mind is the forecasting requirement. Is it going to be necessary to forecast a month ahead or six months? If a forecast for a longer period is required, how much variation from month to month can be tolerated? Once these limitations have been established, various types of averages can be tried out in relation to past data to determine which one or which combination gives the best results.

Control limits

A key element in short-range forecasting is the establishment of control limits. Forecasts are not expected to be completely accurate, but as long as variations are random above and below the forecast, the situation is considered to be in control. It is important to be able to spot variations from the forecast which are not random, but are indicative of a new trend.

Control limits are needed, therefore, to separate the random from the trend variations and to bring to management's attention the fact that a change in the forecast may be required. As long as actual results fall within the control limits, the forecast remains unchanged, whenever the control limits are breached, it becomes an exception requiring a management decision about changing the forecast.

Because of reliance on control limits as indications of normal or abnormal situations, the establishment of the range of control limits for each product forecast becomes crucial. If the limits are too broad, important changes in trends will go unnoticed. If they are too narrow, random fluctuations will give out-of-control signals.

The proper width must be determined on the

basis of (1) analysis of past experience and (2) the effect of variations on production and inventory. An analysis of past data, preferably over at least the last five years, should be made to indicate the extent of past variation. The data should be plotted to determine the trends and seasonal influences during the periods under consideration. A trend line should be drawn, either by inspection or by using the least squares method, and the standard deviation calculated. It may be desirable to establish control limits based on one or two standard deviations; but such control limits should be tested against past data to determine their effectiveness as indicators of changes in trends. It may turn out that a simple percentage, such as ±5 or ±1 per cent of the forecast, will be adequate as an indicator of the control limit.

A key factor in the setting of control limits is the number of periods for which the forecast is required. If a forecast is for the next period only, control limits may be unnecessary, since production can adjust its operations in terms of the changed forecast. If manufacturing needs to plan a level of effort for a period of months and has relatively little flexibility from period to period, it is important that the control limits be so established that significant changes in direction are noted.

Since the primary purpose of the short-range forecast is to permit more effective production scheduling, the particular problems involeved in manufacturing the products being forecast must be taken into consideration in establishment of the control limits. Essentially, control limits are established to make sure that the production plan does not vary from actual requirement by either (1) failing to have the product available to meet demands or (2) increasing inventories to a point where the savings estimated from the length of run are eliminated by the inventory carriyng costs. Inventory levels must, therefore, also be compared with the planned levels to determine whether a situation is out of control . It should be noted, however, that inventory levels are expressed in terms of usage, i.e. number of month, supply, so that the absolute amount of inventory on hand is not indicative of whether the program is in control until it is related to the usage. A decision must be reached as to whether the usage figure used to calculate the number of months' supply will be the monthly forecast figure, the actual demand for the latest month, or some average of the latest month's demand.

The relationship of inventory to the control limits can be taken into consideration by determining how long it would take for an additional average month's inventory to build up if actual requirement continually run close to the lower control limit or, conversely how long it would be before the stock was depleted if requirements continually ran close to the upper control limit.

The variations from month to month are extreme, establishment of wide control limits based on even one standrd deviation might give inadequate control. In such a case, it might be better to establish narrowed limits, but use a short-run moving average rather than only the latest month's data to track actual requirements.

The question of width of control limits is closely associated with actions to be taken when the limits are breached. It is frequently advisable to use closer limits,but not to regard situations as out of control until there have been two successive instances of actual falling outside the control limits in the same direction. The first instance should be brought to management's attention, but probobly no action would be taken if the next period's figures dropped back within the limits.

Case examples

To illustrate how these statistical tools can be used in forecasting, two different forecasting sittuations are described here. The first problem project the demands for some 15,000 items for a small tool company. The second forecasts the demand for approximately 70 different chemicals produced by four major processes.

A Small Tool Company: For the small tool company, the problem was simpler in that the primary concern was forecasting for only one or two months ahead. On the other hand, it was complicated because so many thousands of items were involved. An analysis of the data suggested that the equivalent of a three-month moving average obtained by exponential smoothing best fitted the past data. Averages for the past three months were calculated for each items and the data were fed into a computer. Demand, in terms of monthly shipments for each items, was obtained each month and combined with the previous montly average to obtain a new projected demand. The parts themselves were divided on an ABC—basis the A items being the most important items that accounted for the greatest volume of sales, and items in the B and C categories being less important. The A and B items, which were relatively few in number, were brought to management's attention each month, and, according to rules established the forecast obtained by the statistical procedures outlined would be used for scheduling next month's production unless management decided otherwise. For the C items, production was schedule primarily on the basic of the computed statistical forecast.

A Chemical Company: In the case of the second company, the forecasting of demand was entirely different. A study had indicated that substantial savings could be effected if production could be planned on the basis of a linear programming model.The varied chemical grades could be produced at several plants at different costs, but ony through the use of linear programming was it feasible to determine the optimum method of producing each grade on a continuing basis. Certain savings could be effected simply by scheduling the varied grades on the right units. Substantial additional saving could be realised if it were possible to operate some units at close to 100 per cent capacity and close down certain other units, rather than operating all units at less than capacity. Closing down units was only practical, however, on at least a six months' basis.

To obtain the maximum savings possible through linear programming and effective scheduling, it was necessary to forecast with confidence for six months at a time. A six months' forecast was not necessary, however, for each individual chemical as long as an accurate forecast could be made of the demands for the four different processes by which these chemicals were made. Within these pocess limitations, it would be prossible to change the scheduling of the different chemicals on a monthly basis. The forecasting requirement, therefore, was six months by process and one month by individual chemical.

The first step in the analysis was to determine whether a system could be developed on the basis of past data that would permit accurate forecasting by process on a six months' basis. After some experimentation, it was found that the equivalent in exponentaial smoothing of a seven-month moving average provided the best basis for six months' forecasting. The seven-month average, available early in December and calculated on the basis of the previous moving average and the November shipments, served as a forecast for average monthly demand for the first six months of the year. At the end of each six months' period the forecast for the next months' period would automatically be provided by the latest seven months' moving average.

Examination of the data revealed considerable variation in shipments from month to month. This variation could be absorbed by changes in inventory levels as long as these changes did not constitute more than a month's supply in either direction.

On a trial-and-error basis and influenced by this decision with respect to inventory variation, control limits of plus or minue 10 per cent of the moving average were established. Instead of considering the control limits breached in terms of actual activity or the exponentially determined seven months' moving average equivalent, we used an exponentially smoothed equivalent of a three months' moving average to determine whether we were continuing to operate within the control limits. We made no change in the six months' plan unless control limits were exceeded twice in a row in the same direction.

Over a period of a five years in the past, examination of the data for the major process types indicated that only twice would it have been necessary to have departed from the forecast within any six months' period.

In addition to the control limits around the forecast the monthly inventories were watched closely. Theoretically, it would be possible never to exceed the control limits on the forecast; yet, by continually running close to the same limit over a period of time, inventory could be accumulated or depleted. Therefore, if more or less than a month's supply was added to the selected level of inventory, it would be a signal to change the forecast.

As might be expected, the tracking of the individual chemicals was not as close as for the processes. Since it was possible, however, to make monthly changes with a much less complex linear program for the assignment of chemicals to various pieces of equipment as long as the general process limits were not exceeded, it was found that the tracking of the individual grades was adequate. These grades were tracked in precisely the same manner as the process, with exponential smoothing providing the equivalents of the seven months' and three months' moving averages.

In addition, major customers for each grade and total amounts for major customers for all grades were forecast in precisely the same manner with the same ± 10 per cent limits.

Although the problem will be handled somewhat differently in each company, in most cases the best method of developing a forecasting procedure is to examine past data and determine whether it would have been possible to forecast, based on statistical approaches that are rigidly adhered to.

In most cases, a statistical procedure based on past data should be used in conjunction with information about the market and other external conditions. For example, in the chemical company, on the "basis of past experience it appeared that forecasting would have been sufficiently good, following the statistical procedure indicated, to realize savings through scheduling with linear programming. Because the company already was doing a fine job in examining external factors affecting both industry and company volume, however, it seemed that forecasting could be even better if the statistical techniques described were merged with forecasting procedure previously followed.

Since the use of the moving average for looking ahead six months assumed that the situation existing for the last six months would continue for the next six months, it contained no elements of outside influence. As a result of considering external factors, particularly business conditions generally and the outlook in industries of major importance to the company, its economist at various times in the past had been in a position to indicate that a change in the pattern of sales was likely to take place within the next six months. By combining the statistical average with judgment on external factors, a better estimate than a purely statistical one should be forthcoming. It would be subject to immediate test, however, inasmuch as the control limits would be established as described above and as soon as the forecast got out of control, a signal would be registered.

When a series went out of control, and particularly if it went out of control twice, the economist, the representative of the sales organization, and the representative of the technical staff would all get together and consider what action appeared most desirable. At the meeting they would have information about where and how the process was out of control. In other words, for the general process there would be an indication as to whether it was out of control because of one or two important products or whether all products were going in the same direction. Furthermore, there would be indications as to whether things were out of control because of particular action of one or another large customer or whether, again, the condition was general. Based upon the examination of these data, the sales department's knowledge of why a particular customer or customers were behaving differently from forecast, and its judgment as to what these customers could be expected to do in the next few months, a decision would be made about changing the forecast. In this way, the maximum advantage would be taken of the statistical indicators, the control limits, and the knowledge of the sales and technical organizations as to the reasons for variation from expectation and the possibilities of returning to normal in the future.

Use of seasonal index

In the particular cases described, there were no important seasonal influences that had to be taken into account. If analysis of a company's data shows a regular seasonal pattern, it is necessary to establish a seasonal index and apply it to the figures for the forecast. A monthly average obtained either by exponential smoothing or by the regular moving average process should be adjusted, using the seasonal index, and the data for the coming period should be similarly adjusted in terms of their seasonality. Thus, let us assume that we are starting with a three months' moving average made up of sales of 500 for the month of October, 550 for November, and 700 for December, or an average of 583. We plan to use exponential smoothing from this point on, so our old average is 583.This is influenced by the seasonality of the months in the forecast, so this average must first be seasonally adjusted. We know actual sales for January are 400, and we wish to forecast for February.

Spoyying trends

The primary advantage of using some type of statistical procedure to analyze past data and suggest a figure for the future is the establishment of regular rules to be followed combined with a method for keeping track of the situation continually. An analysis of the past is naturally no guarantee of accuracy in the future, but the use of regular procedure tends to eliminate the possibility of error through varying personal judgments. A systematic analysis of post data at least suggests that changes in the situation will be highlighted and remedial action will be possible. The use of moving average and the variant exponential smoothing tracks the past closely and by the changes in average suggestes changes in trends.

One of the most difficult problems is spotting a trend. The moving average may go for a month or two and may then reverse and go in the other direction. A most important question after there has been an increase in the average for two months is whether this increase is going to continue or is going to be cancelled out by a subsequent decrease. In the example described above, control limits are used as a device to spot changes in trend. As long as averages go up or down within the control limits, no new trend is assumed. If the control limits are breached twice in a row in the same direction, a new trend is suspected but, in the example given, the situation should be checked with the sales departments to find out if there is any information which would be helpful in reaching a decision.

It should be noted, however, that in using the moving averages as we have described them, ifthere is a new trend, the averages will always leg the trend. Under situations where there is a sharp upward trend, for example, a moving average will always be behind because the last figure has only a partial influence on the forecast; the average is heavily influenced by the other month in the computation. The extent of the influence of the last month will depend, of course, on the number of months in the average.

Second-order Systems: It is possible to track an updrown or downward trend more closely with the use of exponentially smoothed averages with a second-order system. Such a system not only show the average in the manner suggested above, but also will make a further adjustment in the new average, depending upon the relation of the new average to the previous one.

In a forecasting program for inventory control purposes, which was established in a company with many thousands of small parts, a study of past data indicated that it would be desirable to have some type of second-order system. The equivalent of a five months' moving average derived by exponential smoothing was used, but the new average obtained at each calculation was furtter adjusted for trend.

N_1 is the new average to be calculated, NC the actual monthly usage in the period, N_2, the old average, and N_3 the previous old average.

In this formula the additional step beyond those described previously is taking one-third of the difference between the latest old average and the old average used in the previous calculation and adding it to the figure for the new average.

This plan was used with a 1401 IBM machine with RAMAC. In this application the change in the new monthly average within one review period was limited to a maximum increase of 100 per cent.

Depending upon the influence desired on the projection, various factors can be used in a second-order system.

Other pertinent factors

A key factor in the use of any forecasting system is the determinant of the proper data to use for comparing actual with forecast. In some companies this determinant wili be shipments; for other companies it will be orders, or something else. The important thing is to use the data that give the best information about what is actually happening to demand requirement. In some cases, orders come in at regular intervals and may be subject to frequent cancellations or changes. In such cases, shipmens may be better indicator. In other cases, orders come in with relative regularity and are not usually changed or cancelled. Since order in all conpaniesprecede shipments other things being equal, orders give the most current information. Sometimes orders or shipments are made to company warehouses andare spaced in some regular predetermined manner that does not give a good indication of actual fluctations in demand. For all these reasons it is important for a company to analyze its own situation and determine what series of data are likely to be most useful for forecasting purposes.

Special problems exist with respect to new products. Where there is no backlog of pripor information upon which to draw, forecasting for new items or new products presents unusual difficulties. Again, it is important to consider the nature of the company's distribution system. A company that sells through a long chain of distributions before reaching the final consumer may be deceived by initial large shipments of a new item because the pipelines are being filled. Before any real indication of consumer demand has been expressed, shipments may be large for several periods and then abruptly cease because the pipelines are filled and the consumers are not buying.

It is possible for such a company, usually through some sampling procedures, to determine what is happening to the products at the consumer level and thus obtain information that can be used to guide production before the effect of consumer buying shows up in distributors' orders.

It my be possible through experience to establish some profile for new product usage by studying the performance of various product at the early stages of their development and comparing the usage proofile of a new product with these established norms.

In additionl to determining the right data to use for forecasting purposes it is also important to decide upon the right usage period to use.In many companies this will be monthly usage; however, in some it may be weekly usage, or even quarterly or semiannual usage for some products.

Through a combination of statistical technique and judgment of those people in the organization closest to customers and markets, it should be possible in most companies to produce forecasts that will permit better production planning. It should be emphasized that important elements in a forecast for manufacturing purposes are (1) forecasts must be specific in terms of the particular units to be manufactured (2) there must be an automatic procedure in terms of rapid feedback of actual result to indicate when the forecast needs adjustment, and (3) control limits should be set around the forecast to permit random variations within these limits without continual change of forecast.

7 Risk Analysis

Introduction

Risk, risk analysis and risk engineering

Risk analysis is often associated with very specific techniques or contexts. For example, a common association is fault tree or event tree analysis in safety assessment. A less common and quite different association is a special case of decision analysis when Monte Carlo simulation is used.

This paper adopts a very general colloquial definition of uncertainty: a lack of certainty. An equally general colloquial definition is used for risk: a significant implication of uncertainty, usually involving potential loss or injury, but sometimes involving gain or other advantages.

Risk analysis can involve a number of approaches to dealing with the problems created by uncertainly, including the identification, evaluation, control and management of risk. Risk engineering is an integrated approach to all aspects of risk analysis, used as the basis of discussion here. Its aim is to identify and measure uncertainty as appropriate, and to develop the insight necessary to change associated risks through effective and efficient decisions. Risk engineering uses risk analysis for the purpose of better risk management.

A broad view of risk analysis is central to the style of risk analysis advocated in this paper. However, colleagues applying it to specific problems in specific organizations often find it useful to employ a name for it which is specific to their own organisation and context, to avoid erroneous asssociations and misconceptions. For example, in project planning one variant of it has been referred to as probabilistc project planning (PPP) and synergistic contingency evaluation and review technique (SCERT).

It is often convenient to use the work risk as a specific short form for 'source of risk' or 'degree of exposure to risk'. However, in the interests of clarity, this paper will avoid such short forms and technical interpretations like "the probability that a particular adverse event occurs during a stated period of time, or rusults from a particular challenge". These are sources of potential confusion to be aware of when reading other material on risk analysis.

A very wide range of contexts can be approached with the style of risk analysis advocated in this paper. For example, areas of application within the oil and gas industry with which the authors have experience include the assessment of project schedule duration, capital cost, operating cost, system and quipment reliability, environmental impact and security, safety, reservoir size, bury depth for pipes exposed to ice ridge scour, other engineering design choices like the selection of a river crossing method, economic viability, financial feasibility, insurance and contractual issues. Other contexts of current or recent interest include the assessment of a variety of risks associated with: computer based accounting systems, hydroelectric power generation, producing and marketing timber products. investing in or lending to a developing country, placing satellites in orbit, and underground construction and tunnelling.

The need for risk analysis

Recent decades have been characterised by a vast proliferation of risk. The real scale of projects and investment programmes has expanded dramatically, increasingly intractable resources have been developed, and economic instability in growth rates and prices has become endemic. With this uncertain and volatile environment, the need for risk analysis of potential projects and investments has increased. The need for analysis is particularly apparent when projects involve:

- Large capital outlays.
- Unbalanced cash flows, requiring a large proportion of the total investment before any returns are obtained.
- Significant new technology.
- Unusual legal, insurance or contractual arrangements.

- Important political, economic or financial parameters.
- Sensitive environmental or safety issues.
- Stringent regulatory or licensing requirements.

In many cases the additional information needed to reduce risk and uncertainty to an acceptable level prior to commencing the development will not be available, and there may be large costs or delays in acquiring it. These factors increase the need for early assessment of the uncertainties and risks which affect the project, before large sums of momey are irrevocably committed.

The requirement for risk analysis

There are five somewhat different circumstances in which uncertainty may be a major factor and in which suitable forms of risk analysis may be appropriate:

- For pre-feasibility appraisal of a proposed project or investment, when a decision must be made, often on the basis of minimal information, to discard the project, to postpone it, or to proceed with more detailed feasibility studies.
- For diciding whether or not to undertake or become involved with a marginal project, when the rate of return calculated on the basis of the best estimates of capital requirements and cash flows is close to the opportunity cost of capital, or the net present value is close to zero.

- When a project or investment involves unusual risks or uncertainties, which may lead to a wide range of possible rates of return.
- For strategic decisions, when choosing between alternative projects or investments, for a project or investment concept which has already been justified at an earlier pre-feasibility or feasibility stage.
- For tactical decisions, when developing a detailed plan or optimising project specifications, for a project concept already given approval.

Within this broad framework, there may be formal requirements for risk analysis for many reasons:

- Ecomonic viability assessment, for high level strategic decision making within the organisation.
- Financial feasibility assessment, for the bond or debt market when a finance package is being assembled.
- Insurance purposes, to assess premiums for unusual risks for which there may be little statistical or actuarial information.
- Accountability, for managers of major projects to demonstrate that they have fully assessed all the material risks, that the measures taken to control risk are appropriate, and that the economic reward for taking on the risk that remains is adequate.

- Contractual purposes, to assess alternative contractual and legal frameworks for the project, in the context of deciding who should bear what risks and determining an equitable allocation of risks and rewards between project owners, contractors and insurers.

- Tendering, when deciding whether or not to bid for a proposed project, and at what level.

- Regulatory purposes, for legislative, judicial or licensing agencies of government, or for public enquiries, to demonstrate accountability in a public or social context.

- Communication purposes, to provide information for project owners, contractors or joint venture partners, or to demonstrate capability and competence in an area.

The benefits of risk analysis

Risk analysis may be required initially for a limited range of purposes. However, the experience of many organisations suggests that it provides other benefits which may prove far more important in the long term. These benefits include:

- Better and more definite perceptions of risks, their effects on the project, and their interactions.

- Better contingency planning and selection of responses to those risks which do occur, and more flexible assessment of the appropriate mix of ways of dealing with risk impacts.

- Feedback into the design and planning process in terms of ways of preventing or avoiding risks.
- Feedforward into the construction and operation of the project in terms of ways of mitigating the impacts of those risks which do arise, in the form of response selection and contingency planning.
- Following from these aspects, an overall reduction in project risk exposure.
- Sensitivity testing of the assumptions in the project development scenario.
- Documentation and integration of corporate knowledge which usually remains the preserve of individual minds.
- Insight, knowledge and confidence for better decision making and improved risk management.

Of these benefits, it is the reduction in project risk exposure which provides corporate management with the bottom-line justification for undertaking risk analysis studies. At the project management level, better insight is the critical aspect, leading to better decision-making and better risk management.

Outline of the paper

The family of models used to deal with such a wide range of situations and objectives is necessarily general, incorporating probability trees in basic and specific forms, decision trees, activity networks, component reliability networks, and Markovian processes.

Five aspects of this approach to risk analysis require consideration: models, computation procedures, methods, method design, and computer software. All five are difficult to separate for discussion purposes. Only partial separation is attempted in the next section which is primarily concerned with models and computation procedures. This is followed by comparatively short sections dealing with some residual method, method design and computer software issues.

North Sea project planning is used to illustrate these aspects. A specific example is essential, and the one chosen is convenient for a number of reasons. However, other contexts are discussed briefly in relation to this example.

The emphasis of the treatment is a particular style of risk analysis, referred to as risk engineering (RE) when a distinction is necessary. This labeal was chosen to reflect an emphasis on a very generl and constructive synthesis of ends and means. Within this RE framework, a particular form of computation procedure is emphasised, referred to as a controlled interval (CI) or a controlled interval and memory (CIM) approach. "However, the next section briefly considers alternative computation procedures, some of which may be desirable within an RE framework, and the final conclusion section comments briefly on other risk analysis frameworks.

The authors make no claim to originality for this paper, in the sense that most of the material covered may be found in a number of their other papers and books, some of the former already published. The purpose of this paper is tutorial, assuming limited familiarity with risk analysis as discussed here. However, the authors hope all readers will gain some new insights, and operational researchers may find some of the material useful for explaining concepts to their clients if and when they find them useful themselves.

Risk analysis models and computation procedures

This section dominates the paper in terms of pages, not because it covers the most important aspects, but because these aspects must be understood of comments on the other aspects to make sense. It draws on one paper published previously, three papers in progress which are available, and two draft books in progress which the authors hope will be available soon, without further individual citations.

Risk analysis is concerned with uncertainty and its consequences. Mathematically, risk analysis models manipulate probalities and probability distributions, in order to assess the combined impact of risks on the project. The exact manner in which this is done depends on the purpose of the analysis.

There is no single all-purpose risk analysis model. Some models are very simple, while others may be very complex, embodying not only uncertainty about events or activities, for example, but responses to that uncertainty and the consequences of the responses. In general it is advisable to start with simple models, and to make them more complex only if doing so seems cost effective.

The next subsection considers a very simple initial model and computation procedure, concerned with the joint duration distribution for two sequential activities with independent individual duration distributions.

Nine following sections consider generalization of this example within the project planning context in five ways: computation, specification, operators, statistical dependence, and model structures.

The next two subsections consider alternative models and alternative computation procedures within the project planning context.

A final subsection considers alternative contexts.

Initial model and computation procedure

An offshore pipeline project might have 'design' specified as the first of a sequence of activities, i = 1...n. Design may be associated with duration D_1 months and probability $P(D_1)$.

The uncertainty might arise from uncertainty associated with the availability of design staff which is not worth more detailed analysis, giving rise to the common slightly asymmetric distribution.

It may be convenient to interpret this uncertainty in one of two quite differnt ways.

One is discrete distribution illustrated by the probability tree. Alternative forms for the same interpretation which are worth noting but not particularly useful are conventional bar histogram representations of the density and cumulative probability distribution functions.

The other way to interpret this uncertainty is as a continuous distribution illustrated by the rectangular histogram probability density function.

Generalization of the specification process

Error associated with the specification of probability distributions is often orders of magnitude more important than that induced by the crudest computation process.

In practice, if the common interval specification is used, more values are usually desirable, normally in the range 4 to 20, to represent the uncertainty in more detail. Any required level of precision of representation may be achieved, trading off specification effort and the benefits of that effort. Appropriate computer software can also generate a detailed specification, normally using 30 to 50 cells, from any convenient and appropriate distribution function and associated parameters. For example, Beta distributions can be used, defined by the minimum, maximum and most likely values, as commonly employed in PERT.

The common interval aspect of the controlled interval could be relaxed. For example, given a generalized CI computation procedure, wider intervals could be used to represent smaller probabilities, in order to reduce computer storage and computation requirements without sacrificing precision of representation of the distribution tails. The desirability of this generalization depends upon the value of precise representation of the tails. It has been deemed not worth the complications it causes in project planning.

Even the controlled aspect of unequal intervals could be relaxed in the sense that it could be ignored for specification purposes, but this may complicate computing and interpretation without significant benefits. Exceptions are truly discrete alternatives constrained to particular values, when it may be necessary to abandon the continuous distribution interpretation, but even these exceptions can be considered within the overall controlled interval umbrella.

The generality of the CI approach from a specification prespective is important in term of controlling specification error, allowing its reduction to a minimal level. However, this clearly does not guarantee freedom specification error,unless a subjective probability prespective which simply ignores the existence of such erro is adopted, an approach not recommended here. More specifically, the $P(D_1)$ values of Figure 1 are associated with a ftrst order probability model for D_1. In a second order model the $P(D_1)$ may have a range of values with associated $P(P(D_1))$,and so on, as indicated by Raiffa. It may rarely prove worth using higher order models explicitly. However, the optimistic bias implicit in assuming $P(D_1)$ are deterministic is always worth bearing in mind.

Generalization of the operator set

In the context of a generalized CI addition procedure, further generalization to subtraction,multiplication, division, greatest, least, and other similar operator is straightforward, in principal if not in practice. The bimodeal nature of this specification makes obvious the two separated underlying cases. Often two or more separate underlying cases are not immediately obvious. Whether or not such separate cases result in multimodel distributions, they are often worth separate identification and estimation, to reduce specification error. Combining these separate cases using associated scenario probabilities requires another useful operator in practical computer software:' weight distributions 1 . . .n by probabilities p_1 . . .Pn.

Generalization to incorporate statical dependence

The procurement activity associated might be followed by a 'delivery' activity associated with uncertainty in a conditional form defined.

The uncertainty represented is explicitly dependent upon procurement duration. This might reflect the past delivery performance of the two different suppliers. Having defin $P(D_b)$as just discused, P(Dc)where $D_c = D_b + D_i$ could computed using the independent addition. In practice it may be more convenient to maintain a 'memory' of D_2 when combining D_1 and D_2, storing a matrix of $P(D_a)$ value by D_2 sourcs instead of collapsing to a single $P(D_a)$ vector, so that D_c can be defind by $D_a + D_3$. This memory concept can be generalized, so that any distribution in a sequence to be operated on can be conditional upon any previous distribution, the 'controlled memory aspect of the CIM approach. However, computational effort increases exponentially as the number of memory dimensions increases, which clearly limits the viability of the CIM computational procedure to small number of memory dimensions.

Examination demonstrates that dependence may involve changes in distribution shape. In practice, change inskey may be involved, and even changes from positive to negative dependence. However, the specification effort associated is such that it may be convenint to replace this format by something simpler if simple unifrom positive dependence is involved. This may be done using appropriate computer software by providing a per cent dependence operator, which operates on unconnditional specifications of the component distributions. The software first combines the distributions assuming independence, corresponding to zero per cent dependence. It combines them again assuming all percentile values of the component distributions coincide, corresponding to one hundred percent dependence.

It then interpolates linearly at the specified percent dependence level. To familiarise a user with what percent dependence dependence. means, the result of the more general procedure of can be illustrated graphically in relation to associated zero and one hundred percent dependence bounds.

In practice it might be better to model 'procurement' plus 'delivery' for supplier A, do the same for supplier B separately, then collapse the associated tree. In general, if statistical dependence can be avoided by transforming it to a structured form it is worth doing so. However ,it is not always possible to avoide dependence in this way. Experience suggests it is often present, despite best efforts to avoid it.If it is simply assumed aways, very substantial error result. Specification errors associated with unconditional distributions like those for D_1 and D_2 have negligible effects upon results compared to incorrect dependence specifications. Hence it is very important to face the statistical dependence issue with as flexible a model and as much determination as possible, after transforming statistical dependence into a structural from of dependence whenever possible.

Model structure generalization: Markov processes through time

The separate treatment of suppliers A and B for the procurement and delivery sequence just discussed could be interpreted as form of model structure generalization. Five further form of model structure generalization are of interest in the present project planning context, the first of which is considered in this subsection.

Following the 'delivery' activity, 220 Km of 32 inch steel pipe may require coating with six inches of concrete and anticorrosive material. Estimation of an associated duration $P(D_4)$might be approached indirectly, via estimation of a coating rate R in km/month and associated probabilities P(R).

The uncertainty reflect productivity variations for a known coating yard operating on single shift basis without any industrial disputes or other significant diffculties. It might be interpreted as a transition distribution, for a simple Markov process, and used to create a sequence of corresponding state distributions.

Whenever a Markov process like this is a reasonably valid represonably of reality, it is representation estimate the equivalent of $P(D_4)$ via P(R), and greater estimation precision can be expection.

The information provided is much richer, and very useful. Knowledge of the stock distribution for all time periods allows consideration of overlap between coating and the following pipelaying activity.

The time period by time period structure is often useful as a basis for the further generalizations of model structure to be considered in the next four sections, although each can be employed without a Markov structure.

Model structure generalization: Responses

The $P(D_4)$ distribution obtained above could be added to $P(D_d)$, $D_d = D_1 + D_2 + D_3 + D_4$. In practice it may be more convenient to incorporate $P(D_c)$ into the initial conditions of the Markov process. This would allow the consideration of a response to delays associated with any previous activity within the Markov process. For example, a second shift might de used for coating, if by time period 14 measure from the planned start of the project less than 100 km of pipe are coated. This would require replacing the state dependent transition distribution with state and time dependent transition distributions variety of decision rules for responses of this kind could be considered. As responses would be used in practice, incorporating them provides a much more realistic picture of duration uncertainty, modelling negative statistical dependence in a causal form, but this is simply a spinoff of a much richer and more useful planning process. If, for example, such modelling suggested that using a second shift was extremely likely, planning for it in advance and undertaking contracts with a second shift was extremely likely, planning advance and undertaking contracts with a second shift provided for might save large amounts of time and money.

Model structure generalization: Sources of risk

When considering the 'pipelaying' activity following pipe coating, it may be useful to start with a focus on a singele source of risk, weather variations.

When weather effects and associated decision rules are understood, further source of risk might be added, one at a time like the laybarge not being when planned, the laybarge not working as fast as planned, and so on.

Model structure generalization: networks

Dealing with the dependence generated by a network structure preceding a merge event is possible via the memory aspect of the CIM approach.

A greatest operation on B and A plus C, followed by the addition of E, determines the finishing distribution for E. Adding A plus D determines the finishing distribution for D. However, a greatest operation when merging these two paths to determine the project finishing distribution must consider their joint dependence upon A. This requires a memory of A through both paths, allowing the final merge to proceed initially in terms of distriubutions which are conditional upon the duration of A, then 'forgetting' the A memory by using the probabilities of specific A durations to remove the condition.

The CIM approach does have clear limitations if a complex structure is involved, and a generalized PERT type algorithm has yet to be defined. However, when modelling activities at a source of risk/response level of detail, it is usual to employ only 20 or so activities to represent a very large project. This means a CIM based approach is usually viable for a detailed risk analysis like that associated with the pipelaying activity, although it could not be used exclusively for a large PERT network.

Model structure generalizations: Stochastic overlaps and precedence relationships

Each of the precedence relationships which define both networks has its own identifiable relationship. This facilitates generalization of the finish-to-start precedence relationships of both diagrams to finish-to-finish and start-to-start relationships. It also facilitates representation of overlaps which may be probabilistic and precedence relationships which may involve alternatives, including alternatives conditioned probabilistically by the performance of earlier activities.

When modelling activities at a source of risk response level of detail, it is usual to employ only 20 or so activities, as noted in the last subsection. This tends to increase the complexity of the precedence relationships. For example, a materials delivery activity followed by a construction activity will involve a stochastic overlap if different materials are involved but not identified, because construction will be affected in different ways by the delayed arrival of different materials.

Alternative models

Within the project planning context, the most obvious alternative is the PERT model. PERT models are effectively special cases of RE models at the level of detail associated with design and procurement. Another alternative is the

Generalised PERT or GERT model. These models are effectively special cases of RE models at the level of detail asssociated with pipe coating. Both alternatives are embedded in a general RE family of models which includes other features not otherwise found in project planning models, although they are found in other contexts. For example, the source of risk/response structure of the pipelaying activity analysis is often used in risk analysis in a safety context. Even the deterministic CPM model is a simple special case.

Although all alternative probabilistic project planning models known to the authors are embedded in RE models, it is worth noting that some deterministic models are not: for example, the basic CPM cost model trading off reduced indirect cost generated by a reduced project duration against increased direct costs to speed up selected activities. These considerations must be incorporated in the method, because they are excluded from the formal modelling process.

Alternative computation procedures

Three alternative computation procedures deserve attention in a project planning context, for rather different reasons.

Monte Carlo simulation could be used wherever CIM procedures are used. However, much greater computation effort is required for the same level of precision unless 'memory' dimensions become numerous. A complex PERT network involving several thousand activities, for example, is better handled via simulation. It is not yet clear where the line of demarcation lies, but an approach integrating both forms of computation procedure would clearly be superior to either on its own.

Mean-variance approaches like the original PERT algorithm could be used effectively whenever the distributions to be added are all sequential, independent, and either numerous or Normal. Similar log-Normal assumptions apply to products. There would be some saving in computation effort. However, such circumstances are very rare, and any significant degree of approximation can induce substantial errors. Other moment-based approaches using higher moments and incorporation dependence overcome some of the restrictions of a meanvariance approach, but by no means all, at considerable cost in terms of conceptual and computational complications. They cannot be used to specify multi-model distributions.

Discrete and approximate numerical convolution procedures for continuous distributions are very similar to the CI approach in their separate ways, and incorporating them produces useful synergy. The memory concept is one spinoff of that synergy not associated with either.

Alternative contexts

Alternative contexts usually involve quite different terminology. For example, in a reliability context 'sources of risk' become 'sources of outage', 'responses' may be limited to 'repair' and duration may become a period of outage translated into 'lost production'.

Alternative contexts usually involve somewhat different model structures. For example, and assessment of alternative ways to cross a river with a large gas pipeline required simultaneous treatment of multiple-criterion measures of the consequences of damage scenarios, in terms of lost gas production, lost production of oil due to loss of an oil line on the same bridge, dollar cost of damage to the bridge and pipe lines, amount of spilled oil, and so on. A further special characteristic of the model structure was the probabilistic transformation of the wide set of initiating event levels into a limited set of damage scenarios.

However, the modelling choices are much the same , a common probabilistic algebra is involved, and some very different circumstances can be catered for with any given model. For example, the pipe coating activity model associated with a production process and inventory model which could be linked to a probabilistic demand model using a structure like that of the pipe laying model. This model could be used to study integrated pricing, advertising, production and inventory policies for a coal mining operation, a timber development, a manufacturer of sail boats, or a producer of children's toys. Sources of variation in production and demand could be considered individually, at various levels of detail, or not at all. Responses to competitive action or industrial disputes or other sources, of variation in demand or production could be linked to specific and general responses or just the latter. Marketing children's toys and laying offshore pipelines involve very different considerations, but common model structures may prove useful.

Although very similar model structures may be involved in very different contexts, an important feature of the RE model set is their generality and flexibility.

No matter how general and flexible a model set, there clearly are limitations. Solutions looking for problems are always a source of risk. The sail boat manufacturer just considered might be better with a dynamic programming model, or a linear programming model, or some other quite different model, if indeed he needs a model at ll.

Risk analysis methods

A technique like critical path analysis (CPA) can be associated with a model (activity network) and a method. Such methods can be perceived as akin to the OR method steps, with two key differences. They are specific to the class of problem being considered, and they are specific to the model to be used. Making them specific in this way limits their flexibility, but increases their efficiency and effectiveness. When designing a new technique, it is important to make the model and method distinction very carefully and to focus attention on their relationship.

Risk analysis methods must be designed to suit the model and the circumstances in which it is used. There is no single all-purpose method for risk analysis. Families of related methods have been developed, involving similar concepts and characteristics. Like the CPA method, they follow a systematic series of steps, but the steps are related to the specific risk analysis context.

When it was tentatively agreed that models like that associated with pipelaying in the last section would be used for offshore North Sea projects, a tentative method outline was developed, tested, modified as appropriate, and documented during the period 1976-77. This method has since been used for about 20 major projects, with some furter minor modifications. It is described in more detail elsewhere. A brief outline will suffice here.

The first phase is qualitative. The project is divided into a very limited number of key activities; each activity is described in detail; a precedence and an associated time scaled bar chart are constructed to show precedence and time relationships; all significant sources of risk associated with each activity are listed and described; all feasible responses to each source of risk are then listed and described. Where appropriate, secondary sources of risk associated with responses are similarly considered. The overall problem structure is then studied, destinguishing responses which are specific to single sources of risk from responses which apply to sets of risks, ordering responses, and studying associated decision rules.

A distinction is mase between minor sources of risk, major sources of risk whode non-realization will be a condition of the quantitative analysis, and major sources of risk to be modelled probabilistically. All project staff with relevant information are involved at appropriate stages, and the problem perception captured by this documentation is agreed with management before the qualitative phase ends.

The second phase is quantitative. The probabilities that risks will occur and the probabilities of various consequences given assumed decision rules for responses are assessed, considering structural and statistical dependencies. The cumulative effect of successive sources of risk is then computed, to provide a portrait of the relative role of each source of risk within an activity, and the relative contribution of each activity total time risk. At intermediate stages in this accumulation process, feedback occurs. Feedback continues until everyone is stisfied with the assumed probabilities and decision rules in relation to the conditions identified earlier.

When the project team is satisfied with the schedule risk analysis, associated cost risk is considered. For example, activity duration distributions are combined with unit of resource per unit time distributions, and probabilistic treatment of exchange rates and inflation rates are used if appropriate. Only when management is satisfied that they have an understandable and justifiable case for all major decisions inherent in this overal result are the associated plans and budgets released.

This method has provided an experience base for the design of a number of other methods explicitly recognizing the model, method and method design distinctions. Some previous OR experience might be associated with these distinctions in retrospect, but explicit recognition is important in the authors' view.

Risk analysis computer software

The first applications of the RE approach in a project planning context in 1977 involved models like the pipelaying example, with detailed consideration of sources of risk, responses, secondary risks associated with responses, secondary responses to those risks, and so on. Pocket calculators were used, to avoid preconditioning the model structure by computer software limitations. However, even with a simple model structure, computer software to perform the computations is clearly desirable.

In 1978 cimmon interval software was developed, with 9 versions incorporating a range of extensions over the period 1978-82. Significant modifications were made to deal with some projects but a range of other projects have employed existing software. A new generation of controlled interval and memory software is now under development, and a micro computer version is under consideration. No single software system will cope with all possible application areas and styles of analysis. However, the new generations of software will be quite general. For current information, please contact the authors.

Other commercially available computer software for risk analysis falls into two main groups. One contains general simulation languages and packages based on Monte Carlo procedures, which could in principle be used to do everything discussed earlier. Such packages would benefit from incorporating a CIM capability,in the authors' view. The other contains specific model or technique based software, like the GERT package marketed by Pritsker and Associates, Monte Carlo based PERT packages, and event and fault tree software. Only certain special cases might benefit from incorporating a CIM capability, like Monte Carlo based PERT packages.

Risk analysis method design

Method design involves choosing or developing an appropriate model/method/software combination for a particular kind of risk analysis in a particular context. The time and money available to perform the analysis, and the expected future use, are obviously important considerations, as will as the immediate task. Method design is a process which is necessarily dependent upon experience and intuition.

A very detailed treatment of sources of risk and responses has important benefits related to all the objectives of risk analysis noted earlier. It also involves considerable expenditure in terms of staff effort and information requirements. However, a method can be designed to make use of simpler models, following a fairly obvious sequence of simplifications, discussed in detail elsewhere.

In other contexts the transformations required of the methods to coincide with revised model structures can be more significant. Some have proven remarkably easy to deal with. Others have required considerable effort.

Other considerations

Risk analysis and specialist expertise

Risk analysis models, methods and software provide valuable tools for project planning and design, but obtaining the right answer still depends upon specialist expertise. Judgments must be made, in some cases based upon hard data, in others based on sound conventional guidelines. In other cases creative innovation and well schooled intuition based upon a wide range of relevant experience must be used. Expertise involving an effective and efficient blend of all these aspects is not made less important by adopting risk analysis methods: it is simply made use of more effectively.

Risk analysis requires many forms of expertise. Economics, finance, environmental issues contractual issues, etc., are clearly involved in most major projects. What is not always appreciated is that they may directly impact the way the design and planning is done, and they should be properly considered in a timely manner. Risk analysis helps to provide this integration.

Risk analysis study team management

Risk analysis study team management requires special consideration. Like the model/method/software aspects of risk analysis method design, it must be adapted to the circumstances. For example, one company uses an in-house Risk Analysis Group in an internal audit role most of the time. Analysis examine a project plan and cost estimates in detail over a period of six to eight weeks. Their work then provides useful immediate feedback to the project staff, but they report to the project manager and the head of the planning and costing function group. Other companies have used large teams over several months to perform a complete analysis, externally to the project team, and to make recommendations based upon fundamental judgments which go beyond the risk analysis itself. Other studies have involved only two or three professionals over an elapsed time of just a few weeks. Very different kinds and styles of management are clearly necessary for such diverse operations.

8 Scheduling of Operations

Organizations operate most efficiently with a smooth, even flow of goods and services passing through them. Unfortunately, the availability of inputs seldom matches the output requirements in either the temporal or spatial dimensions.

Organizations therefore face the task scheduling—of planning physical, spatial, and temporal transformations. Scheduling is the task of specifying when and where certain events are to take place. In the physical conversion of goods, scheduling specifies which individuals and facilities are to be assigned to particular tasks and when these tasks are to be performed. Resources for service operations, such as maintenance and repair, transporting and serving customers, are similarly allocated on a time basis.

The scheduling time horizon

The scheduling process consists of the development of a series of plans or schedules with successively shorter time horizons. Firms forecast and plan conversion to some extent when they determine the proper capacity for and desing factory buildings, warehouses, railroad systems, and so forth. Further scheduling is necessary in the selection of equipment and processes to assure that the processes selected are the most economical for the anticipated level of operations. After facilities are acquired, scheduling at a more detailed level is necessary to plan the best level of operations and employment throughout the year. Finally, monthly, weekly, and even daily schedules are developed to describe in detail the precise activities of individuals and facilities.

Previous sections of the book have dealt with the long-term forecasting and planning involved in the facilities design decisions. In this chapter, we assume that we are looking for the best operating schedules within the constraintrans of existing facilities.

A manufacturing firm producing goods requires two types of operating schedules. The manufacturer needs schedules of the aggregate or total level of production for the intermediate time span of up to 12 months in order to plan for the hiring of people, acquisition of raw materials, and creation of inventories. Short-term schedules of perhaps less than a month's duration are then developed within the confines of the aggregate schedule. The short-term schedules assign individuals and facilities to specific products and orders based upon up-to-date information about orders and inventory levels. Such short-term scheduling typically is labeled production control.

Planning the aggregate production level

The necessity for planning aggregate, production, employment, and inventory levels arises because of uneven time patterns of either inputs or outputs. If inputs were available at a uniform price throughout the year and if sales requirements were evenly spread, the optimal schedule would be to produce at the average demand level with no seasonal inventory buildup and no necessity for hiring and layoff, or for overtime to adjust employment to the production schedule. Unfortunately, most firms contend with some seasonality in the demand for their products. In industries producing products such as boats, toys, lawn mowers, farm equipment, and antifreeze, as much as 80 to 90 per cent of annual sales may occur in substantially less than half the calendar year. Even necessary items such as food and clothing, which have a more stable consumption pattern, often exhibit an appreciable degree of seasonality.

Some organizations also face the constraint of an uneven rate of raw materials input. For example, fruit and vegetable canneries receive all their input of each basic product within an interval of a few weeks out of each year. Firms with seasonal inputs usually have a limited number of production alternatives available. Canneries, for example, must produce all their canned peas within a few week s because of the spoilage rate of the raw material. Such schedules give rise to high cost because the firm must maintain expensive equipment which it uses for only a small part of each year.

The alternatives open to the firm with a seasonal demand pattern are more numerous because of the capacity to transport products over time through the use of inventory. At one extreme, the firm can meet each change in demand with a change in the production rate, accomplishing this by hiring and laying off employees and by the use of overtime and idle time. At the other extreme, the firm can maintain an even production and employment pattern and accommodate the seasonal sales pattern by building up inventories during the slack sales periods and reducing them during the peak times. Other alternatives consist of all combinations of the two extremes, using some inventories and having some variation in the production and employment rates.

Specific penalty costs are associated with all of the alternatives for smoothing production. Level production schedules result in large stocks of seasonal inventories with their related storage and carrying charges. Overtime operations usually require a 50 per cent wage payment premium and result in increased inefficiency when large increments are scheduled. Idtrons time may be even more costly. Changing the employment level may be rrelatively simple in some firms where a low skill level is required, but extremely expensive in firms where several months of training may be necessary in order to bring employees to an acceptable productive level. In addition, a schedule which utilizes a varying production rate will require more capacity than a stable pattern.

It is no simple matter to arrive at accurate cost estimates for hiring, carrying inventory, and so forth, since many of the cost components may be real but intangible economic costs, and others may be allocated jointly among a variety of accounts. The estimation problem is complicated because the costs do not remain constant and may vary considerably over a short period of time. Three critical factors are suggested as determinants of the total incremental costs of changing production and employment levels.

1. The production output rate and inventory and employment levels of the period about to end, that is, the point of departure.
2. The magnitude of the change in the production rate, the employment level and inventory level.
3. The length of the period of the production schedule.

The current operating level represents some point in the total production cost curve of the firm. This cost curve is not a straight-line function; the marginal costs vary throughout the curve. For example, if a firm has been operating at 75 per cent of normal single-shift capacity, a 10 per cent increase in the production rate can be accomplished by hiring more workers. If the firm had been operating at 100 per cent of normal capacity, however, an increase of the same magnitude might require a second-shift operation, and increased supervision in addition to hiring more workers. Similarly, a reduction in the production rate from the 100 per cent level could be accomplished by a small reduction in the work week, or by laying off personnel with the lowest seniority and least skill. If the production rate were down to 50 per cent of normal capacity, however, further reductions in employment might necessitate laying off highly skilled employees whom the firm may not be able to rehire at some later time.

The effect of the magnitude of the change is fairly obvious It costs more to hire and train ten employees than to hire and train one. In fact, it may well cost more than 10 times as much. Normally, a few people with the required skills probably are available in the local labor market. However large increases in the employment level will require more intensive recruiting, covering a widen geographic area and the hiring of some people without the desired skills. Thus, the cost per employe hired will increase as more are hired. The same relationship will hold with respect to reductions in the employment level. There is usually some attrition plus those recently hired who can be layed off at little cost to the firm. Larger layoffs may require some restructuring of the organization and direct penalty costs because of union restrictions and state unemployment compensation laws.

The length of the production schedule affects the choice of alternative methods of adjustment. Some of the costs occur only once while others are imposed over several successive production periods. Consider the alternative of producing a unit during regular time some number of time periods before it will be sold, or of producing it during overtime in the same period that it will be sold. The premium overtime charge occurs just once, whereas an inventory carring charge for the product produced ahead of time will accumulate for each period it is held in storage. It may be less expensive to carry a unit in inventory for a few periods than to produce it during overtime, but the best decision will change if it is necessary to carry the inventory for many time periods.

Planning horizon

Firms typically follow a practice of planning the aggregate production rate for monthly increments for a year into the future. The schedule is based on forecasts of sales. As a result of the deviations between actual and forecast sales, firms must revise the original schedule frequently, perhaps as often as once a month.

Thus, the planned production rate for a specific month may be changed as many as twelve times in the year prior to that month. Despite the frequent schedule changes, the development of schedules for a year into the future is not a wasted effort. Consider what would happen if a one-month time span were used. Starting in January, the schedule which minimizes the total cost for the next one-month period is one in which the production rate matches the demand rate. The same is true for February and the subsequent months. Following this practice, there would never be any buildup of inventory in anticipation of the later peak demand periods. As a result, the schedules in September,October, etc., would be very costly to meet since production would have to match the high demand rates for those months.

The proper objective is to minimize cost over the entire year. A firm must develop a schedule for the next month which is consistent with a minimum cost *yearly* plan. This is not the schedule which minimizes cost for the next month. That schedule would be a suboptimal schedule; it optimizes at a lower—level—the one-month period. The optimal schedule will have higher costs through the early part of the year because of the buildup of seasonal inventory so that the production rate and the costs in the later part of the year can be kept at a reasonable level. Even though this schedulc must be changed frequently, the revisions are usually minor and are made in order to react to deviations in the actual demand from the forecast level to bring the overall yearly plan back into adjustment. The revisions do not invalidate the original schedule, they merely adjust it more precisely.

Linear decision rules for aggregate scheduiling

Firms have used a variety of approaches to determine aggregate production schedules including graphical methods, trial-and-error simulation analysis, and linear programming. A linear decision rule model developed by a research group at the Carnegie-Mellon University helps not only to develop the original schedule but also to modify and adjust it in the light of unforeseen developments.

The linear decision rule model minimizes the total cost of meeting demand over the yearly horizon. It begins with the development of a total cost formula consisting of the variable costs associated with the aggregate schedule. We define the following terms:

P_t = Scheduled production rate in period t

W_t = Work force level in period t

I_t = net inventory at end of period t

S_t = sales forecast for period t

A_t = actual sales in period t

C_t = cost coefficients and system parameters for particular organizations

We find the cost of changing the employment level, by computing the size of the change, $W_t - W_{t-1}$, and squaring it, and multiplying by C_2, a cost coefficient. An organization determines this cost coefficient by estimating the cost of employment changes of varying magnitudes, plotting the values on a graph, and fitting a curve to the points. Trial and error will determine the particular value of C_2 which describes the curve that best fits the points.

The overtime cost expression consists of a series of curves, one for each possible employment level. Each employment level, Wt, has an ideal production rate equal to C_4W_t where C_4 is the average number of units produced per worker per time period. A lower production rate results in an ineffcient use of manpower and a higher rate requires overtime with its increased costs. In overtime cost expression, $C_3(P_t-C_4W_t)^2$, the cost term C_3 is determined in the same manner as the term C_2.

Comparison of the actual inventory level I_t to C_8, the ideal inventory level, determines the inventory cost expression. The ideal inventory level consist of the raw materials, safety stock, inventory in process, and the like required to handle the normal daily transcations If is greater than C_8, the firn will have excessive inventory carrying costs. If is lower than C_8, extra costs will occur because of stockouts, abnormally short production runs, and other delays. The inventory cost expression is $C_7 (I_t—C_8)^2$. The C_7 cost term is determined in the same manner as C_2 and C_3. Note that the terms C_5 and C_6 appear to be missing in the sequence of numbers used. The original linear decision rule model developed by the Carnegie research group included the terms C_5 and C_6 along with C_9,C_{11}, and C_{12} cost terms. The researchers who developed the model used these terms to make the model conform more closely to the actual cost patterns in the firm for which the model was developed. But the terms have been omitted here since they are not essential to the operation and understanding of the model.

Solving the above equation results in a schedule that minimizes costs over the next period. A series of such schedules, each minimizing cost over the next period, is not the same as minimizing total cost over a longer period. Equation 11.1 produces a schedule which would never build up seasonal inventory since there is no dvantage in doing *so for the current time period.* A scgedule that might be more costly in the next period but that will lead to lower costs later is perferable. Thus, a firm minimize total cost over a longer time horizon:

$$TC_T = \sum_{t=1}^{T} TC_t$$

where T is the appropriate time, usually 12 months. Equation 11.2 is subject to the constraint

$$It = I_{t-1} + P_t - A_t.$$

To obtain the scheduling rules that minimize total cost, we differentiate the equation with respect to each decision variable, P_1, P_2, . . .P_{12}, W_1 W_2, . . .W_{12}, and then solve the resulting expressions. We then have a pair of linear decision rules that specify the production and employment levels.

The two decision rules are applied at the beginning of each month. The computations are simple and require only a few minutes to perform. The rules support the kind of behaviour that we would intuitively expect. Both the production rate and the employment rate depend upon future sales, with the immediate future weighted more heavily than the distant future, upon the current employment level, and upon the current inventory position. The terms [153—464_{t-1}] represent the inventory influence on the production rate. If the net inventory level is large, the sum of the two terms in the brackets will be negative thus pushing production downward. If the net inventory level is small, the sum of the two terms is positive and exerts an upward pressure on production in order to bring inventory back toward the desired level.

The application of the scheduling equations to a firm. The firm has had a stable demand of 500 units per month which suddenly increases to 1000 units. Table 11.1 illustrates the optimal schedule when the change was not foreseen. The optimal reaction when the increase is perfectly forecast. The linear decision rules minimize the total cost of reacting to changes in the demand petterns. Obviously, we can develop a more effective schedule when we can anticipate the changes. Thus, by determining the optimal schedule with a perfect forecast and with various degrees of error in the forecast and comparing the costs of such schedules, we can obtain a precise measure of the value of accurate forecasts for future salse. This information may then be used to decide whether it is worthwhile to develop more elaborate and expensive forecasting teachniques in an effort to improve the accuracy of forecasts.

The automatic control feature of the linear decision rules operates through the inventory term. If, for example, sales during period t are 100 units less than forecast,then it will be 100 units more than anticipated. During the next period, the term, will total 46.4 units less than the value if sales had been as forecast, thus reducing production for that period by 46.4 units to bring inventory toward the desired level. The adjustment would continue through the following periods untils inventory is finally at the desired level.

Several published reports indicate that organizations gain sinificant savings by using the linear decision rules. In the paint factory in which the original research was performed the application of the rules over a three-year period using a simple moving average forecast would have resulted in a 7.84 per cent reduction in costs. Even if there were no seasonality or random deviations in demand, there would still be regular payroll cost somewhere in the range of 600 plus. Thus the reduction in true variable Costs is much greater than 7.84 per cent.

Despite its apparent value, the linear decision rule scheduling process has not yet enjoyed wide application. This is partially because of the effort required to obtain accurate cost data to fit into the cost expression. Although this may seem like a reasonable excuse not use the linear decision rule model and other systematic scheduling processes, it is not a valid reason. Any kind of scheduling process, even an intuitive shuffoung around of rates and times is presumably based on at least an informe estimate of relative costs. If no consideration at all is given to costs, the resulting schedules are likely to be far from optimal, no matter how they are obtained. Although the results obtained with the linear decision rule model will improve as the cost estimates become more accurate, it is not essential to have completely accurate cost estimates in order to use the model. The model may be used even when substantial errors in cost estimation exist. The results are still.

Scheduling of conversion operations

After long-range planning decisions have been made to establish the capacity of the operating system and intermediate term plans have established the aggregate level of employment, production, and inventories, an organization then must establish schedules for the conversion of individual units and products which fit into the border plans and constitute an efficient use of its facilities. Short-term operating schedules, with time horizons varying from a few weeks to a few months, form the final step in this scheduling process. This short-term scheduling process is often encompassed within the term "production control" in the firm. At this stage, the firm must look at each individual node and link in the production network and determine the rates and times at which raw materials, components, and subassemblies flow through the network as well as the appropriate levels of inventories and manpower assigned to each product and process.

The operating system at this level of decision making is often extremely complex. For example, When one considers that several dozen or even several hundred different products may be produced by such a system with each product possessing a unique set of inputs and operations and aunique path through the network, the enormity of the scheduling task becomes apparent. It is not surprising that even in well run organiztions, stockouts of products occur and slack time will exist at one node while long lines of products are waiting at another node.

However, even a production system consisting of a single node may present considerable scheduling difficulties when several different products must pass through the system.

In the vast majority of production operating systems, it is uneconomical to try to develop the best or optimal schedule because of the systems' complexity. Even if a firm could determine the best schedule for the next month, the firm probably could not follow the schedule very closely since new inputs are constantly entering the system and even a minor malfunction at one node may produce a substantial chain reaction throughout the entire network of the system. Thus, the development of a reasonable schedule—one that will work fairly well most of the time—is a satisfactory objective.

The criteria or measures of effectiveness that may be used to evaluate the scheduling process include the level of finished goods and work-in-process inventory, the percentage of facility utilization, the percentage of orders shipped on time, the average production time per order, the percentage of stockouts or inventory shortages, and the percentage of time spent in setting up or changing over facilities to produce a different product. None of the above can be used as the sole measure of the production control process; all of them must be kept at a reasonable level. A firm can easily develop a schedule that would excel in meeting any one of the above indicators if the others were ignored. For example, a firm can gain a very low inventory level by limiting the number of orders in process, but that gain would be at the cost of poor facility utilization.

Types of physical conversion systems

A number of different classification schemes have been used to describing physical conversion systems. However, the number of different variables describing a system is so large that no classification scheme is very successful in fitting such a diverse assemblage of systems into a few precise categories. There are, however, a few distinctions between system which should be made. First, systems produce products either to specific order or for stock. If a substantial majority of the customers desiring a product are content with a product of a standard or customary set of specifications of size, color, capacity, and the like, it is usually economical to produce the product in relatively large quantities for stock, that is, before specific orders arrive. Examples of such products are canned peas, electric toasters, bedroom sets, and bicycles. If, on the other hand, each customer has a unique set of product specifications, the manufacturer must wait until the order arrives before production can take place. Examples of this type of product are generators for hydroelectric plants, expensive men's suits, architectural drawings, and false teeth.

The production processes used and the scheduling problems encountered differ considerably between the two classifications. When production is to specific order, the production process must be of a general-purpose rather than a specialized type. Since each order is different from the others, the process must have sufficient flexibility to accommodate the differences. This flexibility requires workmen of a relatively high skill level with the capability of determining their own work methods, setting up equipment, and in some cases even designing some part of the product. The technological needs of production by specific order requires machines and other physical facilities. But the producer uses relatively fewer and less specialized pieces of equipment since the physical equipment does not possess the flexibility of humans to make changes from one order to the next.

When production is for stock, the conversion process can begin and even be completed well in advance of the time the customer decides he wants the product. The process can be automated since it is more repetitive. The human skills requirements are not as great. The workers can be trained to follow closely specified methods and need not deviate sustantially from them.

Scheduling is more difficult when production is to order. With production for stock, a manufacturer can use forecasts of demand to establish production goals. Based on these forecasts, he can determine the requirements for raw materials and purchased components. Since the output is standardized, fewer different kinds of materials are needed. Manpower and facilities may be utilized at a more constant rate; since flexibility exists in the time dimension, conversion need not be tied to specific orders. Movement between nodes in the conversion network may be scheduled in advance. Movement is easier because the products tend to follow a more consistent path through the network and the adjoining nodes in the process can be located next to each other.

Another important classification dimension depends upon sales volume. If the expected sales volume of a product is sufficiently large, production can be accomplished most economically on a continuous basis. A firm may establish a separate set of facilities devoted exclusively to a single product. Substantial economies accure to large-volume continuous production. Highly automated physical facilities can be designed, built, and used for the conversion proess. Although such equipment may reduce the cost per unit of production, the capital cost is warranted only when a sufficiently large volume of sales exists. In addition, no time is lost in starting, stopping and changing over from one product to another. Movement between nodes in the process is minimal and can be handled automatically.

If sales volume is small, production is

accomplished on an intermittent or a jobbing basis because the use of expensive, highly automated facilities is uneconomical. Even less expensive general-purpose facilities must be shared by several products when the volume of each is at a level which utilizes only a small portion of the available equipment time. In a job shop production process, a given department may produce a product for a week and build up sufficient inventory to last for several weeks or months. During the next week, the department produces another product and so on.

Again, the scheduling problems encountered vary considerably between a continuous and an intermittent or jobbing process. In a continuous process, much of the scheduling is built into the design of the process itself. In a continuous process, such as a bottling plant or an automobile assembly line, it is essential that the work load at each node or each work station be equal. The slowest station limits the speed of the process. Since each station is closely linked to the whole process, a slow down at one station will delay the entire process. This balancing of the work load takes place at the time the process is designed and after that little scheduling is necessary. We will examine the line balancing problem in more detail later in this chapter.

In a discontinuous process, all the problems of coordinating the conversion of several products in the same facilities exist and the scheduling task is formidable for even a relatively simple system.

At this point the reader can appreciate the difficulty of trying to fit individual organizations into exact categories. Some products are produced to order and others for stock, or part of a product may be produced on a for-stock basis with other stages in the process taking place only after a specific order has been received. Similarly, a given organization may produce some products continuously, others discontinuously, and others partially with both types of processes. Also, some products may be produced continuously by one organization and discontinuously by another depending on the individual organization's sales volume. Thus, our method of classifying conversion systems represents, at best, simply a way of looking at the factors determining how conversion should take place and the kinds of scheduling problems encountered in each kind of process. This will be useful in examining the production control problems and the scheduling techniques used to handle them.

We have insufficient time and space to try to consider scheduling of every type of conversion process. We can, however, examine a few of the more interesting cases. We will consider first the line balancing problem of the continuous production process. Secondly, we will look at a single-node system with discontinuous production for stock. Next, we will consider how we can attempt to schedule conversion on a complex multi-node system with discontinuous production both for stock and to specific order. Finally, we will look at some of the problems of estimating the processing times used in the scheduling process.

The line-balancing problem

In a continuous production system with a separate set of facilities devoted to a single product, the primary scheduling problem is to obtain the desired level of output with the minimum input of labour and other resources. For example, an automobile assembly line may be set up with a pace of operation to produce a finished automobile every 60 seconds. The scheduling task is to assign the work in a manner which minimizes the number of work stations and workers required to perform all the assembly operations within the 60 second time period. Work assignment scheduling is not done for each individual unit, but the schedule is built into the structure of the conversion process, and the assignment of individual tasks to specific work stations remains the same until the structure of the entire process is changed.

The first step in balancing the line is to define the job-and the work tasks constituting it. We define work tasks as the smallest meaningful segments of work which can be assigned to an individual work station. Any further subdivision will result in substantial additional work. In defining the tasks we also specify their sequence requirements. Each task has some time relationship with all other tasks. It either must precede or follow, or it is indpendent of the performance of every other taks. The network suggests, for example, that task b cannot be started until a is completed; b must be done before d can be started, and b can occur either before or after c. The figures below the nodes give the average task performance time in minutes.

Consider now the assignment of the task to work stations. The total time available at each station depends on the required output of the process which in turn depends on the expected sales or usage rate of the output. In the example above, suppose that a unit must be produced every 1.0 minutes. Tasks a and d, if combined, would fall within the 1.0 minute time limit. They cannot be assigned to the same station, however, since tasks b and c must be performed between a and d. Thus, the job would require five separate work stations. This results in a rather low labour utilization level. The total amount of actual work accomplished is equal to the sum of the task times, or 3.4 minutes in this case. However, five workers are occupied for 1.0 minutes each for a total labour time of 5.0 minutes or a labour utilization rate of 3.4/5.0=.68.

In practice, it might be difficult to achieve even this level of output. The time figures given for each task represent the average performance time. Considerable variation in the time requirement for each task may exist from unit to unit. There may be some variation in the specific work involved in a given task from one unit to the next. For example, on an automobile assembly line, each automobile is somewhat different than the next in terms of body, transmission, and engine configuration as well as in the number and kinds of special accessories. The average time for installing a transmission may well vary with the kind of transmission.

In cases where the product specifications and the work assignments remain exactly the same from unit to unit, variations in time requirements still exist. Some inherent and unavoidable variation exists in the time in which the work is completed owing to a variety of causes such as parts being slightly out of proper shape wear in tools, accidental dropping of parts, or simply because the workers change their pace.

When the production process is rigidly paced as it is when the product moves along a conveyer line, the effect of this variation is substantial since the rigid pace ties all the work stations together. Suppose that on two successive units the worker on task b requireds 1.1 and .7 minutes respectively, while the worker on task e requires .5 and 1.1 minutes during the same two cycles. Even though each was working at this average pace, the line could move only after all workers completed their work on a given cycle. In this case, the line could move only after 1.1 minutes on each cycle. The longer the line, the more serious is the time variation problem.

It becomes very difficult to achieve high labour utilization on a continuous process system because of the limited divisibility of work tasks and variation in the processing times. Fortunately, there are ways of reducing the effect of these obstacles. Back-up operators are sometimes used. Their job is to step into the line at points where the individual operator is falling behind. Also, inventory can be used to partially decouple the work station. A bank of goods in process between stations can absorb many of the variations in time from unit to unit instead of having the repercussions felt immediately throughout the entire line.

Despite the problem of balancing the line, the continuous process has economic advantages, such as reduced materials handling, smaller facility and tool investment, and lower skill requirements, that can be achieved when sales volume is sufficiently large. Since such systems exist, they must be designed and scheduled. Much work has been done to develop models that produce optimally balanced lines. We will consider first a method useful in handling problems of moderate size and then consider a model for handling very large problems.

Rules for balancing assembly lines

The first method for balancing an assembly line uses two fairly simple rules to assign tasks to stations:

1. construct all possible combinations of tasks at each succeeding stage;
2. eliminate combinations when:
    a. all tasks in one set are contained in another; or
    b. when one different task exists in a combination set but requires less time than the task in another set and does not

permit the inclusion of any different subsequent task combination at sueceeding stages.

The line balancing problem is a combinatorial problem, that is, one of seeking the right combination among many possible combination of assignment of work tasks. Rule number 1 forms all possible combination. Its use alone would be sufficient and would assure that the best solution was obtained. However, the number of different combinations is exceedingly large for even moderately sized problems, and rule 2 helps to reduce the number of alternatives under consideration by eliminating those alternatives for which others equally good or better exist.

Cycle time is 10 minutes. The sum of the task times is 46 minutes. Thus, at least five work stations will be required. The reader can verify the usefulness of the systematic rules at this point by attempting to balance the line by inspection. The optimal five stations solution is not easy to see.

At stage 1, the list of alternative combinations becomes:

(a b c)

(a b h)

Neither can be eliminated by rule 2

Stage 2: (a b c) fh

(a b c) gh

(a b c) ih

(a b h) cf

(a b h) cg

(a b h) ci

The last 3 combination sets contain the same work tasks as the first 3 sets and can be eliminated by rule 2(a). We apply rule 2(b) to comparison of the first and second sets with the differing tasks f and g. The first set can be eliminated since f requires less time than g. In comparing the second and third sets, neither can be eliminated since differing tasks i and g have different succeeding tasks which might be included in subsequent stations.

Stage 3: (abc, ih) fj

(abc, ih) g

(abc, gh) i

(abc, gh) fd

Applying rule 2(a) eliminates the third set.

Stage 4: (abc, ih, fj) gd

(abc, ih, g) fj

(abc, ih, g) fd

(abc, gh, fd) i

(abc, gh, fd) e

Computer method for balancing lines

The number of possible combinations increases rapidly with problem size. Although the previous set of balancing rules will always produce the best solution, the rules become too unwidely for lines with a large number of tasks. For large complex products, several hundred separate work tasks must be performed. An interesting and useful approach for balancing large lines is through the use of COMSOAL, which is an acronym for Computer Method of Sequencing Assembly Lines. This process uses a high-speed digital computer to generate a random sample consisting of a large number of solutions. Even though the probability is very small that any one of the solutions is optimal, there is a reasonably good chance that at least one of the solutions generated will be optimal if a large enough sample is taken. As we will see, the probability of obtaining an optimal solution can be calculated precisely.

This problem with eight tasks has 112 different feasible ways of combining the tasks. One or more of the combinations requires the minimum number of stations; one or more, the minimum number plus one; and so on.

Distribution of Feasible Sequence Combinations for COMSOAL

Stations Required	Number of Sequences
4	25
5	84
6	3
Total	112

Suppose that a process generates random

feasible sequences and that *r* is the proportion of the universe of feasible sequences which require the minimum number of stations. The probability that the first sequence generated will be optimal is r and the probability that it is not is (1-r). If n sequences are generated, the probability that all are non-optimal is $(1\text{-}r)^n$, and Pn, the probability is $1\text{-}(1\text{-}r)^n$ that at least one sequence drawn is optimal. Pn approaches 1, absolute certainty, as n increases even when r is very small.

We must know the value of r in order to compute Pn. Unfortunately, r rarely can be determined with precision. In our example, r=25/112=.223. In this case, we enumerated all possible sequence combinations, a task that is obviously impossible for large-scale problems. Although no short cut exists to determine r, a reasonably good solution would normally suffice in a practical problem. We can hypothesize that an economic sample will, in most cases, contain at least one optimal sequence, and that in the comparatively few cases that possess a very small r, at least one sequence in the economic sample will require only one station in excess of the optimal number.

The problem of rapidly and economically generating sequences still remains. COMSOAL uses a process which involves progressive selection of tasks from among those which have no unassigned preceding tasks. The COMSOAL approach for our problem is:

Step 1: From an availability list which includes all task which now have no preceding unassigned task.

Step 2: Form a fit list which includes those tasks from the availability list which require times equal to or less than the time left available in the station to which work is now being assigned.

Step 3: In the simplest form of COMSOAL, a random selection is made from the fit list and task is assigned to the work station to which work is now being assigned.

Steps 1,2 and 3 are repeated until all tasks have been assigned. The result is a sample of size 1. Addditional solutions are generated by repeating the generation process until the desired number of solutions have been generated. The randomness of the selection process in step 3 assures that a different solution will result in each successive run.

The COMSOAL generating process we have described was improved by biasing the selection of tasks from the fit list instead of selecting them at random. A total of nine different biasing rules were tested which tended to favor the slection of fewer station combinations, thus tending to increase increase r, the probability of generating an optimal sequence. Among the more effective biasing procedures were:

RULE 1. Weight tasks that fit in proportion to task time. The effect of this rule is to give large task a greater chance of assignment early at each station and in the entire sequence. This leaves the shorter tasks to the end. The time space is filled efficiently by loading the longer time spans first and leaving the smaller time spans to fill the reduced time spaces.

RULE 2. Weight tasks that fit in proportion to the number of immediately following tasks. This rule increases the chances of selection of tasks which will lead to an expansion of the availability list.

The computer time requirements of COMSOAL can be estimated from Arcus' examples. He found that a 45-task problem generated optimal 8-station assignments in an average of 32 seconds of time on an IBM 7090. He states that Chrysler Corporation implemented an earlier version of COMSOAL and that for a 1000 task job, a 203 station sequence resulting in 1.48 per cent idle time was computed in about 2 minutes of 7090 time.

Having found a computing procedure that produced optimal or near-optimal solutions for basic line-balance problems, Arcus proceeded to provide for a series of other more realistic constraints on the program. In essence, these constraints affect the fit list which must satisfy the new constraints in addition to those stated earlier. These additional constraints will not be described in detail, but the following lists should serve to describe their general nature:

1. Tasks larger than the cycle time
2. Tasks that require two men.
3. Tasks fixed in location

4. Space for parts
5. Time to obtain a tool
6. Time for the worker to change position
7. Time to change the position of a unit.
8. Grouping tasks by criteria
9. Wages related to tasks.
10. Worker movement between units being assembled.
11. Mixed production on the same line.
12. Stochastic task performance times.

Scheduling of multiple products through a single facility

There are a large number of production processes which intermittently produce several different kinds of products for stock on the same set of physical facilities. For example, oil refineries or chemical processing plants may produce one product or a set of products for two weeks during which inventories of these products are built up. At the end of two weeks, processing facilities are used to produce other products and sales demand for the first set of products is met by the inventory which was previously accumulated. It may be several months before the first set of products is produced again. Similarly, an assembly line in an appliance factory may assemble dishwashers one week, clothes dryers the next, stoves the following weeks, and so on. The lack of sufficient sales volume of any single product to justify its owns separate process necessitates the sharing of facilities.

Despite the very common occurrence of this type of production process, no one has yet devised a method for determining the optimal production schedule. To illustrate the scheduling complexities which are introduced by facility sharing, we will attempt to develop a schedule for a very simplified situation, one in which two products share a process.

There are two products A and B with the following characteristics:

	d	p	S	C	i
A	10,000	25,000	$6,000	$10	.20
B	10,000	25,000	$3.000	$20	.20

where

d = annual rate of demand

p = annual rate of production

S = cost of setting up or preparing for a production run

C = cost per unit of producing the product

i = cost of carrying inventory per year

The only remaining problem is to try to fit the production runs for both products into the time schedule of the single facility that must produce both. Either A or B could be produced at the start of the year. We will arbitrairily schedule B first. Product B will be produced for 50 days. During that period 5,000 units will be produced and .2 of the year's demand or 2,000 units will be sold leaving an inventory accumulation of 3,000 units on hand at the end of day 50. This inventory is 3,000/10,000 = .3 of a year's supply and should last until the end of day 125. Thus, the second production run for product B must begin on day 126.

The production process is now available for producing product A from day 51 through day 125, and from day 176 through day 250. Despite the fact that 150 days are available, no single segment is long enough for the 100 days of production that product A requires. We can try scheduling A at the start of the year or try maneuvering the schedule around in other ways, but there is no conceivable schedule which will allow both A and B to be produced at the quantities Q_{PA} and Q_{PB} with each production run beginning at the time inventory for the respective product has just been depleted.

Q_{PA} and Q_{PB} minimizes the sum of the ordering and setup costs only when they are combined into a feasible schedule on the same process. Since a feasible schedule cannot be arranged using those quantities, some type of workable compromise schedule must be developed. We see, that if product *A* were produced in 50-day runs of 5,000 units each, the run could be fitted into the periods between the runs of product B. This compromise, however, would increase the sum of the setup plus carrying costs for product A. With Q_{PA} = 10,000 and Q_{PB} = 5,000, the total annual carrying and setup costs for each product are $12,000 for a total of $24,000 for both products. Changing the production quantity of A to 5,000 units increases the total annual carrying and setup costs for product A to $15,000, or a total of $27,000 for both products.

Another feasible schedule would result if each product were produced once per year in quantities of 10,000 units. *A* could be produced from day 1 through day 100, and product *B* from day 101 through day 200. Such a schedule leaves the total annual carrying and setup costs for product *A* at $12,000, but increases the cost for product b to $15,000, for a total of $27,000 for both products.

Actually, any schedule that calls for the same number of production runs for all products produced on the same facility will be a feasible schedule, no matter how many products share the facility or how many runs of all the products are made per year provided, of course, that the facility has sufficient production capacity. Such a schedule would work even if demand for the several products required that the process operate every day of the year. This is in sharp contrast to the first schedule that we tried in the above example where the process operated at only .80 of full capacity, but still could not produce at Q_{PA} and Q_{PN} because of time overlaps. A schedule for producing each product the same number of times per year will be feasible, and it will not have time overlaps on the facility because each run of each product is offset from the previous run of that product by the same time span. Thus, if the number of runs per year is three, then the second run of product A will begin exactly one-third of a year after the first run began, and so on for products *B*, *C*, and all the rest although the quantities produced of each product and the time required to produce each product varies considerably from one product to the next.

The production of all products which are made by the same facility the same number of times per year may not necessarily be the optimal schedule. It is, however, a workable schedule and may be as close as possible to the optimal schedule in a practical case. If a producer were to operate such a schedule, he would attempt to determine the best value for the number of times of production per year.

Economic production cycle

We can usually analyze and determine the value of N mathematically. The total cost equation to be minimized, which was developed for a single product. The basic differences are that we must now state costs in terms of N rather than in terms of QP and we must sum the costs for all products together.

Variation in the rate of demand

In an actual system, the operation of a schedule such as we have determined may be difficult for any extended time period. The above schedule assumes a rather constant rate of demand. Although we have discussed a situation in which products are for stock, the predicted level of sales and the rate of depletion of inventories are developed from sales forecasts. These forecasts are inevitably in error as the rate of demand changes over time due to causes that are not entirely predictable. Even a small increase in the rate of demand for a single product can have an enormous effect on the production schedule. Suppose, for example, that a production system is scheduled to produce four different products three times a year, with the length of each production run being one month or 20 working days. Product A is produced in January. At the end of January, sufficient inventory of product A has been built up to last 60 more working days until A again is scheduled for production starting in May. However, at the beginning of February the sales rate for product A increases by ten per cent. Therefore, inventory of product A is depleted in approximately 54 working days. If the cost of being without a stock of product A is sufficiently large, a new production run of A will have to be started immediately. This will cut into the schedule of product D, which is normally produced for 20 days in April, after only 14 days of production. As a result, the inventory buildup of product D is insufficient to last the normal 60 working days until D is next scheduled for production. Since only. 70 (14 days/20 days) of the normal production run occurred, the accumulated inventory will last only about .70 x 80 = 56 days from the start of the run. Thus, D would be in a stockout condition 16 days after the beginning of the production run of product B. At this point, the firm may cut short the run of B and switch to product D. In 4 more days, product C has run out. The implication of this adjustment and the snowballing effect of the first small increase in demand is obvious. A firm may easily find itself in a position of continually reacting to the latest crises and rapidly shifting production from one product to another as a result of an initially small change in the normal demand pattern. At a result, setup costs are excessive and stockouts still continue to occur at a high rate.

Index